God
    Has Many Names

BOOKS BY JOHN HICK
Published by The Westminster Press

God Has Many Names
The Myth of God Incarnate, *edited by John Hick*
Truth and Dialogue in World Religions:
  Conflicting Truth-Claims, *edited by John Hick*

GOD
HAS MANY NAMES

by
JOHN HICK

THE WESTMINSTER PRESS
Philadelphia

BOOK DESIGN BY DOROTHY ALDEN SMITH

Published by The Westminster Press®
Philadelphia, Pennsylvania

PRINTED IN THE UNITED STATES OF AMERICA
9 8 7

Library of Congress Cataloging in Publication Data

Hick, John.
   God has many names.

   Contains some material from the author's work with the same title published: London : Macmillan, 1980.
   Includes index.
   1. Christianity and other religions.   2. Religion—Philosophy.   I. Title.
BR127.H53   261.2   82-1959
ISBN 0-664-24419-X   AACR2

Contents

Preface

Christians have always lived, consciously or unconsciously, in a religiously plural world. In some places and periods they have been acutely aware of other religious traditions living and growing alongside their own. But in Western Christianity this pluralistic consciousness has only fully emerged during the lifetime of people now living. Prior to that, religions such as Hinduism and Buddhism, Judaism and Islam, were generally seen as strange and dark residues of paganism, utterly inferior to Christianity and proper targets of the churches' missionary zeal. Today, however, we have all become conscious, in varying degrees, that our Christian history is one of a number of variant streams of religious life, each with its own distinctive forms of experience, thought, and spirituality. And accordingly we have come to accept the need to re-understand our own faith, not as the one and only, but as one of several.

At one level such a change of viewpoint need not be difficult. American Christians, for example, can without raising difficult theological issues extend to the people of other religions the general principle of tolerance and mutual respect which is an accepted cultural ideal, enshrined in the Constitution.

But there is a deeper level of Christian response at which serious theological problems inevitably arise. The prevailing self-understanding of our own tradition sees it as having a uniqueness and finality which make it superior to all others. Indeed, its superiority has been assumed to be such that, in the words of Karl Barth, Christianity "alone has the commission and the authority to be a missionary religion, i.e., to confront the world of religions as the one true religion, with absolute self-confidence to invite and challenge it to abandon its ways and to start on the Christian way." (*Church Dogmatics*, I/2, p. 357.) This sense of unique Christian superiority is grounded in the faith that the founder of the Christian way was none other than God incarnate. That belief accordingly keeps coming to the center of discussion in the course of this book; and it is also examined more fully in *The Myth of God Incarnate* (John Hick, ed.; Westminster Press, 1977). The proper conclusion seems to me to be that the notion of a special human being as a "son of God" is a metaphorical idea which belongs to the imaginative language of a number of ancient cultures. The Christian tradition, however, has turned this poetry into prose, so that a metaphorical son of God became a metaphysical God the Son, second Person of a divine Trinity; and the resulting doctrine of a unique divine incarnation has long poisoned the relationships both between Christians and Jews and between Christians and Muslims, as well as affecting the history of Christian imperialism in the Far East, India, Africa, and elsewhere. As religious metaphor, however, the incarnational language provides a familiar way of expressing our discipleship to Jesus as Lord (the one whom we seek to follow) and Savior (the one who has initiated our eventual transformation into perfected children of God). And part of our theological task today is to re-understand the doctrine of the incarnation along such lines as these, so as to do justice to Christian experience without thereby doing injustice to Buddhist, Hindu, Muslim, Jewish, and other religious experience.

But this work of Christian re-understanding is only part of the larger task of forming a global conception of the relationship between the religious traditions—as also of secular life outside those traditions—to the transcendent Reality which the great faiths all in their different ways affirm. The need here is for a theory which allows us to see, and to be fascinated by, the differences as well as the similarities between the great world faiths. Accordingly it must not set up a pressure to think that the religions all conceive of the Real in the same way, or all produce the same human response to the Real, or all have the same expectations concerning our human future beyond this life. But at the same time it must be true to the basic awareness of our time that in all the great traditions at their best the transformation of human existence from self-centeredness to Reality-centeredness is taking place; so that they can be seen as embodying different perceptions of and responses to the Real from within the different cultural ways of being human.

Some of the chapters of this book begin to explore the outline of such a theory. They are offshoots of my major concern during recent years, which is the development of such a theory in systematic detail. This work continues actively, and my hope is that critical responses to the present small book may enable me to achieve a more adequate development of the theory in the larger book. In the meantime I am already grateful to colleagues at Claremont—John Cobb, Masao Abe, and others—for invaluable help in the course of discussions of the problem of religious pluralism, a problem which has become increasingly central to the philosophy of religion today.

I am grateful both to my wife, Hazel, and to my graduate assistant, Harold Hewitt, for reading the proofs and making the Index.

J. H.

The Claremont Graduate School
Claremont, California

Acknowledgments

I am grateful to the editors or publishers of the following journals and books for their permission to reprint (sometimes in revised form) papers originally published under their auspices:

"Pilgrimage in Theology," from the *Epworth Review*, May 1979, and "Pluralism and the Reality of the Transcendent," from *The Christian Century*, Jan. 21, 1981, and reprinted in *Theologians in Transition*, edited by James M. Wall and published by The Crossroad Publishing Co., 1981, are reprinted here as Chapter I. "Whatever Path Men Choose Is Mine," from *The Modern Churchman*, Winter 1974, is Chapter IV.

"Sketch for a Global Theory of Religious Knowledge," from *Vardag Och Evighet: Festskrift till Hampus Lyttkens*, edited by Bo Hanson, Jarl Hemberg, and Catharina Stenquist (Lund: Doxa, 1981), is Chapter V. "Towards a Philosophy of Religious Pluralism," from *Neue Zeitschrift für systematische Theologie und Religionsphilosophie*, Vol. 22, Part 2 (1980), is Chapter VI.

"Christian Theology and Inter-Faith Dialogue," delivered as the second Younghusband Lecture at King's College, London, on May 3, 1977, under the auspices of the World Congress of Faiths and published in *World Faiths*, Autumn 1977, and also delivered as a lecture at the quincentenary celebrations of Uppsala University in September 1977 and published in *The Frontiers of*

Human Knowledge (Uppsala, 1978), is Chapter VII. "God Has Many Names" (Chapter III) was delivered as the twenty-seventh Claude Goldsmid Montefiore Lecture at the Liberal Jewish Synagogue, St. John's Wood, London, on October 16, 1980.

I
A Spiritual Journey

There are, I suppose, two main kinds of theology, which have been aptly labeled "dogmatics" and "problematics." Dogmatic theology (which need not, however, be dogmatic in the sense of being assertive and unreasoning) studies and conserves the inherited tradition, having accepted its fundamental structure as permanently valid, because divinely revealed. Problematic theology, on the other hand, takes place at the interfaces between the tradition and the world—both the secular world and the wider religious world—and is concerned to create new theology in the light of new situations. Thus while dogmatic theology assumes that its basic positions represent the final truth, problematic theology sees its conclusions as hypotheses, open to revision and always seeking greater adequacy, being comparable in this respect with the hypotheses of the sciences. The first kind of theological thinking provides the ballast and the second the sails of the ship of faith. Being all-too-human, the two types of practitioner have always tended to be suspicious of one another; but in fact both are necessary, the one to keep the vessel upright and the other so that it may be carried onward before the winds of history.

I

My own work lies more in the area of problematics than of dogmatics. To see why, a brief excursion into religious autobiography may perhaps be forgiven.

For a few years at least, as children, we were taken each Sunday to the local Anglican parish church; and the services were a matter of infinite boredom. But although the church had nothing directly to do with it, I have from almost as early as I can remember had a rather strong sense of the reality of God as the personal and loving lord of the universe, and of life as having a meaning within God's purpose. When I was eighteen I read a book called, I think, *The Principles of Theosophy* (a Western version of the Hindu Vedantic philosophy) and felt strongly the attraction of the first comprehensive and coherent interpretation of life that I had encountered. But, although impressed, I was nevertheless not quite convinced by it, and at a certain point I consciously rejected it as being too tidy and impersonal. Nevertheless I was in a state of spiritual searching. The Eastern religious world, in the form of theosophy, was attractive, but not sufficiently so for me to enter it. The Western religious world of Christianity was all around me but seemed utterly lifeless and uninteresting. However, the following year, as a law student at University College, Hull, I underwent a spiritual conversion in which the whole world of Christian belief and experience came vividly to life, and I became a Christian of a strongly evangelical and indeed fundamentalist kind. I was in the company of some fellow students of the Inter-Varsity Fellowship, with whom I had many discussions; and I read the New Testament and was struck with immense force by Jesus' parables and sayings, the story of his life, and the impression of his personality as living lord and savior. I can remember well a period of several days of intense mental and emotional turmoil during which I was powerfully aware of a higher truth and greater reality pressing in upon my consciousness and claiming my recognition and response. At first this intrusion was highly unwelcome, a disturbing and challenging demand for nothing less than a revolution in personal identity.

But presently the disturbing claim became a liberating invitation and I entered with great joy into the world of Christian faith. At this stage I accepted as a whole and without question the entire evangelical package of theology—the verbal inspiration of the Bible; creation and fall; Jesus as God the Son incarnate, born of a virgin, conscious of his divine nature, and performing miracles of divine power; redemption by his blood from sin and guilt; his bodily resurrection and ascension and future return in glory; heaven and hell.

Intending now to enter the Christian ministry, I joined the Presbyterian Church of England (mainly because this was the church to which my Christian friends belonged) and went to Edinburgh for the first year of a philosophy degree course before, as a conscientious objector, joining the Friends' Ambulance Unit for the duration of the war. At Edinburgh I was a keen member of the Christian Union, attending virtually all its Bible studies, prayer meetings, and talks, and engaging in such evangelistic activities as ward services in Edinburgh Infirmary. And yet while greatly valuing and benefiting from the close Christian fellowship of the C.U., I was already beginning to sense in it a certain narrowness and a lack of sympathy with questioning thought. And on returning to Edinburgh after the war, although as emphatically a Christian as before, I did not rejoin the C.U. Nevertheless I continued for many years to be, in general, theologically rather conservative. Indeed one of the first articles that I published (in the *Scottish Journal of Theology* in 1958) was a criticism of the Christology of D. M. Baillie for failing to express the full orthodox faith—an article to which his brother, John Baillie, immediately replied. However, I later, after some fifteen years of new experiences and further reflection, reached a position which is very like that of the Baillies in *The Place of Jesus Christ in Modern Christianity* and *God Was in Christ*. And while I can still enter imaginatively into the conservative-evangelical thought world through which I once passed, and can appreciate and respect the traditional orthodoxy which I once fully shared, I would not now wish to return from the larger to a smaller vision. I can also remember my own resentment at those who raised awkward questions which might upset the established orthodoxy and can understand the similar resentment obviously felt by some more traditional churchmen and theologians today. But I believe that anyone who is either born or "born again" into the conservative-evangelical thought world, and who has a questioning mind, will find that he has to face challenges to the belief system within which his Christian faith was first made available to him, and that he will almost certainly be led by rational or moral considerations to modify or discard many of its elements. The response to Jesus Christ as one's lord, and as one's savior from alienation from God, may remain the same; but the body of theological theories associated with it in one's mind will usually change, and surely ought to change, in the light of further living, learning, and thinking.

II

Indeed my own experience, working in philosophical theology, has been one of continually expanding horizons as the investigation of one problem has brought another, larger problem into view. When I wrote my first book, *Faith and Knowledge*, first published in 1957, I never expected to write another. I thought that I had said all that I had to say. But presently the theodicy issue, the question whether the reality of suffering and wickedness are compatible with the reality of a loving God, was insistently demanding a response; and the result was another book, *Evil and the God of Love* (Harper & Row, 1966). This built upon the epistemology developed in *Faith and Knowledge*, particularly in the notion of "epistemic distance" and in the notion of faith as a fundamen-

tal expression of human freedom. I realized more fully in
the course of writing this book that the kind of theology
at which I was arriving has a long and respectable
ancestry, going back through Schleiermacher ultimately
to the earliest fathers of the church, particularly Iren-
aeus, after whom I have therefore named it. The tracing
of this lineage has been very helpful. For many people
consider a theory more likely to be true if it, or something
like it, was propounded by great figures in the past. And
indeed in a sense no doubt it *is* more likely to be true. At
any rate it is encouraging to find that one's own hard-won
view of things was also the view seen by other and
greater minds in earlier ages.

But another major challenge to religious faith was now
looming up over the horizon, namely that posed by the
diversity of apparent revelations. If what Christianity
says is true, must not what all the other world religions
say be in varying degrees false? But this would mean that
the large majority of mankind, consisting of everyone
except the adherents of one particular religion, are walk-
ing in darkness. Such a conclusion would be acceptable
within a Calvinist theology, according to which much,
perhaps most, of the human race is already doomed to
eternal damnation (*Westminster Confession*, III, 7). But
in wrestling with the problem of evil I had concluded
that any viable Christian theodicy must affirm the ultimate salvation of all God's creatures. How then to reconcile the notion of there being one, and only one, true
religion with a belief in God's universal saving activity?

A move at that time to Birmingham, England, with its
large Muslim, Sikh, and Hindu communities, as well as
its older Jewish community, made this problem a live
and immediate one. For I was drawn into the work which
is variously called "race relations" and "community
relations," and soon had friends and colleagues in all
these non-Christian religious communities as well as in
the large black community from the Caribbean. And
occasionally attending worship in mosque and syna-

gogue, temple and gurdwara, it was evident to me that essentially the same kind of thing is taking place in them as in a Christian church—namely, human beings opening their minds to a higher divine Reality, known as personal and good and as demanding righteousness and love between man and man. I could see that the Sikh faith, for instance, is to the devout Sikh what the Christian faith is to the sincere Christian; but that each faith is, naturally enough, perceived by its adherents as being unique and absolute. Visits to India and Sri Lanka, amounting together to nearly a year, mainly to study Hinduism and Buddhism, further revealed something of the immense spiritual depth and power of these two oriental religions. Without ever being tempted to become either a Hindu or a Buddhist I could see that within these ancient traditions men and women are savingly related to the eternal Reality from which we all live.

A valuable clue to an understanding of the world religious situation came from Wilfred Cantwell Smith's important book, *The Meaning and End of Religion,* first published in 1962 and already now a modern classic of religious studies, with its convincing critique of the concept of "a religion" and of the notion of religions as contraposed sociotheological communities. We ought instead to think of the religious life of mankind as a continuum within which the faith-life of individuals is conditioned by one or other of the different streams of cumulative tradition. From this point of view it is not appropriate to ask, Which is the true religion? For a true relationship to God may occur in the lives of people in each of the great religious traditions. With the problem in its older and insoluble form having thus been dismantled, it was possible to develop (in *God and the Universe of Faiths;* London: Macmillan & Co., 1973; St. Martin's Press, 1974) the idea of a "Copernican revolution" in our theology of religions, consisting in a paradigm shift from a Christianity-centered or Jesus-centered model to a God-centered model of the universe of faiths. One then

sees the great world religions as different human responses to the one divine Reality, embodying different
perceptions which have been formed in different historical and cultural circumstances.
This paradigm shift involves a reopening of the Christological question. For if Jesus was literally God incarnate, the second Person of the holy Trinity living a
human life, so that the Christian religion was founded by
God-on-earth in person, it is then very hard to escape
from the traditional view that all mankind must be
converted to the Christian faith. However, the alternative possibility suggests itself that the idea of divine
incarnation is to be understood metaphorically rather
than literally, as an essentially poetic expression of the
Christian's devotion to his Lord. As such, it should not be
treated as a metaphysical truth from which we can draw
further conclusions, such as that God's saving activity is
confined to the single thread of human history docu-
mented in the Christian Bible. The alternative approach,
which sees the incarnational doctrine as a basic metaphor, is supported by a variety of considerations arising
in the modern investigation of Christian origins; and
others had reached essentially the same conclusion from
the point of view of New Testament and patristic studies.
Accordingly a group of us met for occasional discussions
to write what became *The Myth of God Incarnate*,
intending to bring the idea of divine incarnation, which
had long been something of a shibboleth in British
church circles, back into the light of rational discussion.

III

It is sometimes said, polemically, that nonincarna-
tional theology leads to detachment from the problems of
society, leaving the field open to politically reactionary
or even fascist forces. I am inclined, however, to think
that the opposite is true and that in general, though with

many individual exceptions, a conservative theology tends to be associated with conservative political attitudes and a liberal theology with liberal political attitudes. However, it is unfortunately true that in Britain only a small minority of churchmen and theologians of any persuasion are actively expressing their faith politically, and it is hard to know to what extent these correlations hold true within that minority. There are highly orthodox Christians—for example, churchmen of the splendid Anglo-Catholic socialist tradition—as well as radical Christians engaged in the present struggle to build a successful pluralist Britain, free from racial discrimination. I have certainly found myself that in multicultural, multiracial, and multifaith Birmingham the acceptance of all human beings (and not only fellow Christians) as children of God, and the acceptance of the other great world religions (and not only Christianity) as having their own spiritual validity, involves activity of a broadly political kind, seeking through the work of various organizations to implement these attitudes in such areas as religious education in the schools, provision of places for Muslim, Sikh, and Hindu worship, attention to the needs of the ethnic minorities in hospitals, prisons, etc., and to their treatment by the local media, the relations between the churches and the non-Christian religious communities, structural manifestations of color prejudice and discrimination, the problems faced by black youth and their relations with the police, opposition to the National Front and other fascist and neo-Nazi organizations, etc. These activities, which have taken up a good deal of time during the last twelve years, are as much an expression of my own kind of Christian faith as is going to church on Sunday.

Returning from politics to scholarship, the really exciting theological tasks of the future, as I see them, do not lie so much in the further retrospective study and refinement of one's own tradition (although this should always continue as one activity among others) as in larger comparative and intercultural studies, ultimately on a world scale. At the practical level, this does not mean the emergence of a single world religion. For the different religious traditions, with their complex internal differentiations, have developed to meet the needs of the range of mentalities expressed in the different human cultures. So long as mankind is gloriously various—which, let us hope, will be always—there will be different traditions of religious faith with their associated forms of worship and life-style. The concrete particularities forming a spiritual home in which people can live—the revered scriptures, the familiar liturgical words and actions, the stirring music, the framework of creedal belief, the much-loved stories of founder, saints, and heroes—must continue in their separate streams of living tradition: for in losing their particularity they would lose their life and their power to nourish. But, as human productions, these spiritual homes are all inevitably limited and imperfect, each having its own distinctive strengths and weaknesses, advantages and disadvantages. And in the new ecumenical age which we are now entering, the religious traditions will increasingly interact with one another and affect one another's further development, enabling each to learn, we may hope, from the others' insights and benefit from the others' virtues.

But while there cannot be a world religion, there can be approaches to a world theology. For if awareness of the transcendent reality that we call God is not confined to the Christian tradition, the possibility opens up of what might be called (for want of a better term) a global theology. Christian theology consists in a body of theories or hypotheses designed to interpret the data of Christian experience. Analogously, a global theology would consist of theories or hypotheses designed to interpret the religious experience of mankind as it occurs not only within Christianity but also within the other great streams of religious life, particularly the nontheistic traditions, including large sections of Hinduism, Buddhism, Confucianism, and Taoism, and also within the great nonreligious faiths of Marxism, Maoism, and Humanism. The project of a global theology is obviously vast, requiring the cooperative labors of many individuals and groups over a period of several generations. The increasing dialogue of world religions is basic to this work. Out of this there may be expected increasingly to come comparative and constructive studies both of particular areas of belief and of larger systems of belief. Thus my own discussion in *Death and Eternal Life* (Harper & Row, 1977) is intended as a Christian contribution to a global theology of death, exploring both the differences and the deeper convergences of insight on this subject between Christianity, Hinduism, and Buddhism. This kind of endeavor is both extremely demanding and extremely exciting, but is at present in its infancy and can only develop fully through collaboration between scholars possessing a wide range of expertise.

And so the pilgrimage continues and mingles with many other spiritual pilgrimages which have started at different points throughout the world but are converging in the awareness of a common human history and a common human relationship to the mysterious transcendent reality which we in the West call God.

IV

Let us call the ultimate object of religious worship, experience, and contemplation the Eternal One—a phrase which draws upon associations both with the mystical "One without a second" of the Upanishads and the "Holy One" of the biblical and other theistic faiths. The basic problem in the philosophy of religion is that of the reality of the Eternal One—in traditional Western thought, of the existence of God. There is here a continuity between the concerns of confessionalism and those of pluralism. In either case the basic issue is that of the reality of the Transcendent. And so the opposition in which I engaged in the previous decade against noncognitive analyses of religious language—for example, that drawn from the later work of Wittgenstein—has continued during the last ten years. Believing that such analyses are untrue to the actual intention of religious language users, I still want to consider and evaluate the grounds on which human beings believe in a reality in which being and value are one. Impressive attempts have been made to show that the affirmation of such a reality is a necessity for rational thought. Two such attempts, the ontological and cosmological proofs, have had important revivals in recent years. The arguments involved are complex and fascinating, and I have spent some time with them in *The Many-Faced Argument* (Macmillan Co., 1967), in collaboration with the late Arthur McGill of Harvard, and *Arguments for the Existence of God* (Herder & Herder, 1971). But the "bottom line" can, I believe, only be that none of the traditional theistic arguments finally succeeds. However, it must surely be significant that none of the great world religions was in fact launched by philosophical arguments. Such reasonings were developed later in the course of communicating or defending what was already believed on other grounds. Nor can those other grounds be reduced to belief on the authority of someone else, some great spiritual leader; rather they must be the grounds on which such spiritual leaders themselves believed. And these grounds are in the area of religious experience. The conviction of the reality of the Transcendent, when it is based in religious experience, is an acknowledgment of a presence or a power which impinges upon someone's consciousness, whether gently or traumatically, so that to deny it would be an act of spiritual suicide. Given such firsthand awareness of the divine, the appropriate philosophical apologetic is a defense of the rationality of trusting and living on the basis of compelling experience of this kind. Without attempting to develop it here, I believe that such an apologetic is possible. In Christian terms, its conclusion is that one who experiences his life, in greater or lesser degree, as being lived in the presence of God as made known to us by Jesus is rationally entitled to believe in the reality of that God and to proceed to live accordingly. But if such an argument holds for the Christian experience of the divine, it must also hold for the Jewish, the Muslim, the Hindu, the Buddhist, and other experiences of the divine. One must follow the Golden Rule and grant to religious experience within the other great traditions the same presumption of cognitive veridicality that one quite properly claims for one's own.

It is at this point that we meet the problem of the very different and apparently conflicting reports of the divine coming from the different religious traditions. Can the Eternal One be at once the Adonai of Judaism, the Father of Jesus Christ, the Allah of Islam, the Krishna and the Shiva of theistic Hinduism, the Brahman of advaitic Hinduism, the Dharmakaya or the Sunyata of Mahayana Buddhism, and the Nirvana of Theravada Buddhism? If we presume the basically cognitive character of religious experience within the great traditions, we shall, I believe, be led to draw a distinction between, on the one hand, the Eternal One in itself, as the infinite Reality which exceeds the scope of human thought, language, and experience, and, on the other hand, the Eternal One as experienced, thought, and expressed by finite human creatures. We shall then study the differences between our human ways of experiencing and thinking the divine. For, in Thomas Aquinas' dictum, "The thing known is in the knower according to the mode of the knower" (*Summa Theologica*, II/II, Q. 1, art. 2); and in religion there seem to be many communities of knowers with different though overlapping modes of cognition. Human experience is structured by concepts, and it would seem that one or the other of two basic concepts provides the framework of religious experience. One, which presides over the theistic forms of religion, is the concept of God, or of the Eternal One as personal. The other, which presides over the nontheistic forms of religion, is the concept of the Absolute, or of the Eternal One as nonpersonal. (It should, incidentally, be noted that both forms of religious awareness appear within each of the great world traditions, though in different modes and proportions.) But these very general categorial concepts do not as such form the actual experience of individuals and communities. These ideas take more concrete or particular forms as specific images or "pictures" of God, or as specific concepts of the absolute. Thus the general idea of deity has been concretized in Hebrew experience in the image of Yahweh as a personal being who exists in interaction with the Jewish people. He is a part of their history and they are a part of his. But Yahweh is different from, say, Krishna, who is a distinctively Hindu *persona* of the Eternal One in relation to the Vaishnavite community of India. Again, the basic concept of the Absolute is particularized in different ways within the different nontheistic traditions. This fact is, however, not readily accepted within those traditions. Their customary claim is that in the mystical state of perfect enlightenment there is a direct awareness of reality itself, undistorted by our human cognitive machinery with its variety of images of a personal deity. But in fact the different methods of meditation, the different scriptures feeding the spirit, the different philosophies and sustaining communities, combine in the major Eastern traditions to produce different experiences of the ultimate reality. Thus the distinctive Zen experience is characteristically different from, for example, the distinctive advaitic experience. Here also, then, it seems that "The thing known is in the knower according to the mode of the knower."

This kind of attempt to find a global, or multifaith, epistemology of religion generates its own further questions. For example, it is obvious in principle that some perceptions of the Eternal One may be more accurate and some responses more adequate than others. Indeed, when we take account, not only of the great world faiths but also of primitive religion and of the innumerable smaller—and in some cases eccentric, repulsive, horrible, or destructive—religious movements of the past and the present, it is clear that we do in fact apply moral and other criteria in our reactions to them. What, then, are the proper criteria for judgment in this area? Again, what account is to be given of the nonreligious ideologies, particularly Marxism, by which so many live today? There is thus a plentiful agenda of problems for the religious pluralist.

V

But let me now turn to the effects which a pluralist view of religion has upon one's understanding of and relationship to one's own tradition. However imperfectly (and in fact very imperfectly) this is reflected in my own life, I feel irrevocably challenged and claimed by the impact of the life and teaching of Jesus; and to be thus decisively influenced by him is, I suppose, the basic definition of a Christian. How then is my Christian faith changed by acceptance of the salvific character of the other world religions?

The older theological tradition of Christianity does not readily permit religious pluralism. For at its center is the conviction that Jesus of Nazareth was God—the second Person of a divine Trinity living a human life. It follows from this that Christianity, and Christianity alone, was founded by God in person on the only occasion on which he has ever become incarnate in this world, so that Christianity has a unique status as the way of salvation provided and appointed by God himself. If this claim is to have real substance and effect, it follows that the salvation thus made possible within Christianity cannot also be possible outside it. This conclusion was drawn with impeccable logic in the Roman dogma *Extra eccle-siam nulla salus* (Outside the church, no salvation), with its nineteenth-century Protestant missionary equivalent (Outside Christianity, no salvation). But in the light of our accumulated knowledge of the other great world faiths this conclusion has become unacceptable to all except a minority of dogmatic diehards. For it conflicts with our concept of God, which we have received from Jesus, as the loving heavenly Father of *all* mankind; could such a Being have restricted the possibility of salvation to those who happen to have been born in certain countries in certain periods of history?

But perhaps salvation is not the issue. Perhaps salvation is taking place, not only within Christianity but also outside it, while the unique Christian gospel is that God became man in Jesus to make this possible. The doctrine of atonement thus becomes central. This suggestion appeals to some as a means of acknowledging God's saving work throughout mankind while retaining the dogma of the unique centrality of Christ as the only savior of the world. But in doing so it sacrifices the substance of the older position. For the nerve of the old dogma was the imperative which it generated to convert all people to faith in Jesus as their lord and savior: "No one comes to the Father, but by me" and "There is salvation in no one else, for there is no other name under heaven given among men by which we must be saved." That nerve is cut when we acknowledge the other great world religions as also areas of divine salvation. The other kind of attempt to have it both ways, exemplified by Karl Rahner's picture of devout persons of other faiths as "anonymous Christians," is too manifestly an ad hoc contrivance to satisfy many. For it is as easy, and as arbitrary, to label devout Christians as anonymous Muslims, or anonymous Hindus, as to label devout Hindus or Muslims as anonymous Christians.

Because such responses are inadequate, it seems to me necessary to look again at the traditional interpretation of

Jesus as God incarnate. Such a reconsideration is in any case required today by the realization that the historical Jesus almost certainly did not in fact teach that he was in any sense God; and also by the fact that Christian thought has not yet, despite centuries of learned attempts, been able to give any intelligible content to the idea that a finite human being, genuinely a part of our human race, was also the infinite, eternal, omnipotent, omniscient creator of everything other than himself. The proper conclusion to draw, as it seems to me, is that the idea of divine incarnation is a metaphorical (or, in technical theological language, a mythological) idea. When a truth or a value is lived out in a human life, it is a natural metaphor to speak of its being incarnated in that life. Jesus lived in full openness to God, responsive to the divine will, transparent to the divine purpose, so that he lived out the divine agape within human history. This was not a matter of his being of the same substance as God the Father, or of his having two complete natures, one human and the other divine. Agape is incarnated in human life whenever someone acts in selfless love; and this occurred in the life of Jesus to a startling and epoch-making degree. Whether he incarnated self-giving love more than anyone else who has ever lived, we cannot know. But we do know that his actual historical influence has been unique in its extent.

This kind of reinterpretation of the idea of divine incarnation is, in different forms, fairly widespread today (more so, I think, in the United States than in Britain) and provides, as it seems to me, a basis for a form of Christianity which can be part of the religiously plural world of today and tomorrow.

II
The Christian View
of Other Faiths

The traditional Christian attitude to other faiths was formed in a period of substantial ignorance of the wider religious life of mankind, and it has recently been thrown into a ferment of rethinking by greater and more widespread knowledge.

We can distinguish three phases so far in the development of the Christian attitude to the other world religions.

1. The first phase—the phase of total rejection—was expressed in the dogma that non-Christians, as such, are consigned to hell. As the expression of an attitude to other human beings the dogma is as arrogant as it is cruel; and it is a sobering thought that such a dogma was at one time almost universally accepted among Christians. In the medieval formulations, Christians were of course equated with those acknowledging the supremacy of the Roman pope. Thus we read in a papal pronouncement of Boniface VIII in 1302: "We are required by faith to believe and hold that there is one holy, catholic and apostolic Church; we firmly believe it and unreservedly profess it; outside it there is neither salvation nor remission of sins. . . . Further, we declare, say, define and proclaim that to submit to the Roman Pontiff is, for every human creature, an utter necessity of salvation." (Denzinger, *Enchiridion Symbolorum Definitionum et Declarationum de Rebus Fidei et Morum*, 29th

ed., No. 468f.; Freiburg, 1952.) Again, the Council of Florence (1438–45) affirmed that "no one remaining outside the Catholic Church, not just pagans, but also Jews or heretics or schismatics, can become partakers of eternal life; but they will go to the 'everlasting fire which was prepared for the devil and his angels,' unless before the end of life they are joined to the Church" (Denzinger, No. 714).

The Roman Catholic Church today has passed decisively beyond this phase, but the earlier dogma still persists within evangelical-fundamentalist Protestantism. For example, one of the messages of the Congress on World Mission at Chicago in 1960 declared: "In the years since the war, more than one billion souls have passed into eternity and more than half of these went to the torment of hell fire without even hearing of Jesus Christ, who He was, or why He died on the cross of Calvary." (*Facing the Unfinished Task: Messages Delivered at the Congress on World Mission*, Chicago, Ill., 1960, ed. by J. O. Percy, p. 9; Wm. B. Eerdmans Publishing Co., 1961.) The main difference between the medieval Catholic dogma and this is that whereas the former assumed that Christians are those owing obedience to the pope, the latter is inclined to doubt whether the pope and his followers are Christians at all!

This entirely negative attitude to other faiths is strongly correlated with ignorance of them. There was of course contact in the medieval period between Christianity and Islam; but it was a military contact, not a religious dialogue or a mutual exploration of one another's spirituality. The average Christian's distorted conceptions of Islam were matched only by the average Muslim's distorted conceptions of Christianity. Today, however, the extreme evangelical Protestant who believes that all Muslims go to hell is probably not so much ignorant (for he has some missionary contact with Islam, and an enormous literature is available about the world religions) as blinded by dark dogmatic spectacles through which he can see no good in religious devotion outside his own group.

But the basic weakness in this attitude of rejection lies in the doctrine of God which it presupposes. If all human beings must, in order to attain the eternal happiness for which they have been created, accept Jesus Christ as their Lord and Savior before they die, then the great majority of humanity is doomed to eternal frustration and misery. For the vast majority of those who have ever been born lived either before Christ or outside the range of his historical influence and could not respond to him with saving faith. To say that such an appalling situation is divinely ordained is to deny the Christian understanding of God as gracious and holy love, and of Christ as the divine love incarnate. Thus the attitude of total rejection, expressed in the dogma that outside Christianity there is no salvation, implies a conception of God radically questionable from the standpoint of Christian faith.

2. The second phase—which I shall call the phase of the early epicycles—arose out of a growing awareness among Catholic thinkers of the reality of religious faith, first among Protestant Christians and then among devout men of the great non-Christian religions. The response was to retain the words of the established dogma but to add a rider reversing its practical effect. The dogma thus stands that only Catholics can be saved (*Extra ecclesiam nulla salus*), but it is declared of various people who, empirically, are not Catholics that they may nevertheless, metaphysically, be Catholics without knowing it! There is an analogy here with the dogma of transubstantiation: to human observation the bread and wine remain bread and wine, but their metaphysical substance is said to become that of the body and blood of Christ. Likewise, devout Protestants, Jews, Muslims, Hindus, etc., may remain Hindus, Muslims, Jews, and Protestants, and themselves believe that this is what they are, but they

may nevertheless—metaphysically—be redeemed members of the mystical body of Christ. They may belong to the invisible, as distinguished from the visible, church; or they may be invincibly, and therefore nonculpably, ignorant of the truth of the Catholic faith, and so disposed that they *would* accept it if they genuinely encountered it; or they may have implicit instead of explicit faith; or they may have been baptized by desire, namely their sincere desire for the truth even though they do not yet know what the truth is; or, in a Protestant variant, they may belong to the latent as distinguished from the manifest church.

These are all variations on a common theme. We see the theme being deployed in, for example, the allocution of Pope Pius IX in 1854: "It must, of course, be held as a matter of faith that outside the apostolic Roman Church no one can be saved, that the Church is the only ark of salvation, and that whoever does not enter it will perish in the flood. On the other hand, it must likewise be held as certain that those who are affected by ignorance of the true religion, if it is invincible ignorance, are not subject to any guilt in this matter before the eyes of the Lord" (Denzinger, No. 1647). Or again, in the important 1949 letter from the Holy Office in Rome to the Archbishop of Boston: "To gain eternal salvation it is not always required that a person be incorporated in fact as a member of the Church, but it is required that he belong to it at least in desire and longing. It is not always necessary that this desire be explicit. . . . When a man is invincibly ignorant, God also accepts an implicit desire, so called because it is contained in the good disposition of soul by which a man wants his will to be conformed to God's will." (*The Church Teaches*, pp. 274f.; St. Louis and London: B. Herder Book Co., 1955.)

I call these supplementary concepts epicycles because they are strongly reminiscent of the epicycles that were added to the old Ptolemaic picture of the universe, with the earth at the center, in an attempt to accommodate increasingly accurate knowledge of the paths of the planets. The heavenly bodies were all supposed to move in concentric circles around the earth. This was at one time a plausible theory as regards the stars; but the planets' paths, as they became known, did not conform to the scheme. However, instead of abandoning the scheme the ancient astronomers added a series of smaller supplementary circles, called epicycles, revolving with their centers on the original circles. If a planet was thought of as moving on one of these smaller circles, while it was in turn moving around the great circle, the resulting path was more complex and nearer to what was actually observed; and this complication of the system made it possible to maintain the basic dogma that our earth is the hub of the universe. In theory it was possible to stick indefinitely to the faith that the earth is the center, adding epicycle upon epicycle to reconcile this theory with the facts. However, such a system became increasingly contrived and burdensome; and the time came when people's minds were ready for the new Copernican conception that it is the sun and not the earth that is at the center. Then the old Ptolemaic picture was thrown aside and was soon seen in retrospect as utterly antiquated and implausible. It may well be that much the same will apply to the Ptolemaic theology whose fixed point is the principle that outside the church, or outside Christianity, there is no salvation. When we find persons of other faiths to be devout, we add an epicycle of theory to the effect that although they are consciously adherents of another faith, nevertheless they may unconsciously or implicitly be Christians. There is no point at which such maneuvers become logically impossible; but nevertheless their intellectual cost can mount to an unacceptable level.

3. During the last few decades, and particularly since Vatican II, a third phase, which we may call that of the "later" epicycles, has been evident. Here theological ingenuity goes to its limits to hold together the two

propositions that outside Christianity there is *no* salvation, and that outside Christianity there *is* salvation! The
second of these propositions acknowledges an evident
fact. For if the idea of salvation is given any experiential
content, in terms of, for example, human renewal, liberation, re-creation, becoming a new creature, or achieving
an authentically human existence, then it is manifestly
the case that such transforming experiences occur outside as well as inside Christianity. Accordingly, the first
proposition has had to be reinterpreted to bring it into
harmony with the second. This is achieved by tacitly
converting it from a factual assertion into a stipulative
definition. Instead of being the assertion that only Christians can be saved, it becomes the definitional conven-
tion that all who are saved are to be called Christians—
not, however, directly, but under some oblique description. For example, Karl Rahner has contributed the
notion of "anonymous" Christianity. "Christianity," he
says, "does not simply confront the member of an extra-
Christian religion as a mere non-Christian but as someone who can and must be regarded in this or that respect
as an anonymous Christian." (*Theological Investigations,* Vol. 5, 1966, p. 131; London: Darton, Longman &
Todd; New York: Seabury Press.) This seems a bold and
world-ecumenical utterance; and yet, on analysis, it does
not in substance go any further than the early epicycles.
The anonymous Christian is the invincibly ignorant man
of implicit faith, who is baptized by desire, and who
therefore belongs to the invisible church. However,
Hans Küng's more daring proposal looks like a genuine
advance. He distinguishes between the ordinary way of
salvation within the world religions and the extraordinary way within the Catholic Church. "A man is to be
saved," he says, "within the religion that is made available to him in his historical situation." (In Joseph
Neuner, ed., *Christian Revelation and World Religions,*
p. 52; London: Burns & Oates, 1967.) Thus the world
religions are, he says, "the way of salvation in universal

salvation history; the general way of salvation, we can even say, for the people of the world religions: the more common, the 'ordinary' way of salvation, as against which the way of salvation in the Church appears as something very special and extraordinary" (Neuner, p. 53). The orbit of Küng's epicycle is now so wide that it is in danger of flying off out of the Ptolemaic frame. For if "ordinary" were taken to mean "majority," and "extraordinary" to mean "minority," we should have a straightforward acknowledgment that most men are saved by God through religious traditions other than Christianity. However, Küng makes it clear that this is not his meaning. For him the ordinary way of salvation through the world religions is only an interim state until the adherents of those religions arrive at an explicit Christian faith. People of other faiths, he says, "are pre-Christian, directed towards Christ. . . . The men of the world religions are not professing Christians but, by the grace of God, they are called and marked out to be Christians" (Neuner, pp. 55–56). The non-Christian's right and duty to seek God within his own religion is only "until such time as he is confronted in an existential way with the revelation of Jesus Christ" (Neuner, p. 52). Thus it is clear that this is not a Copernican revolution in the Christian theology of religions but only another epicycle, sophisticated and charitable but still confined within the traditional Ptolemaic mold.

Another form of later epicycle, more readily available to the liberal Protestant than to the Roman Catholic or the evangelical fundamentalist, removes the traditional this-life restriction, and declares that although all men must sooner or later accept Christ as their Lord and Savior, they may still do this in the life to come, if they have not done it in the present existence. This is in some ways an attractive theory, though still not without its own difficulties. For if salvation is recognized as a present human experience, then it undoubtedly occurs outside Christianity as well as within it; and if salvation for the non-Christian is confined by our dogma to the world to come, we have a clash between dogma and fact.

It is understandable that a growing number of Christians seem to have lost confidence in all these theological epicycles and are open to the possibility of a Copernican revolution in our Christian attitude to other religions.

The Copernican revolution in astronomy consisted in a transformation of the way in which men understood the universe and their own location within it. It involved a radical shift from the dogma that the earth is the center of the revolving universe to the realization that the sun is at the center, with all the planets, including our own earth, moving around it. And the Copernican revolution in theology must involve an equally radical transformation of our conception of the universe of faiths and the place of our own religion within it. It must involve a shift from the dogma that Christianity is at the center to the thought that it is *God* who is at the center and that all the religions of mankind, including our own, serve and revolve around him.

I have already acknowledged that it is possible in principle to go on indefinitely thinking Ptolemaically. But we have to realize that a Ptolemaic type of theology is capable of being operated not only from within Christianity but equally from within any other faith—just as men on Mars or Jupiter, if there were any, could formulate their own Ptolemaic astronomy, with their own planet as the center of the system. The most striking non-Christian example of this today in the religious realm is provided by contemporary philosophical Hinduism. This holds that the ultimate reality, Brahman, is beyond all qualities, including personality, and that personal deities, such as the Yahweh of the Bible or the Krishna of the *Bhagavad-Gita,* are partial images of the Absolute created for the benefit of that majority of mankind who cannot rise above anthropomorphic thinking to the pure Absolute. Thus the various religions of the world, with their different proportions of anthropomorphism and mysticism, can be seen as so many approaches to the truth that is fully revealed in the Upanishads. Here we have a Ptolemaic system with a Vedantic instead of a Christian center. And from this point of view the Christian, the Jew, the Muslim, or other devout person can be said to be a Vedantist without knowing it. He is an "anonymous" Vedantist; he stands within the lower or "ordinary" realms of the religious life, but will rise eventually into the "extraordinary" realm of the truly enlightened; he is a Vedantist "implicitly" and by virtue of his sincere desire for the truth, even though he does not yet know what the truth really is; although in error in this life, he will be confronted by the truth in its full glory in the life to come and will then be converted to it. Thus all the epicycles of Ptolemaic Christianity can also be used to maintain a Ptolemaic Hinduism—or a Ptolemaic Buddhism, or Islam, or Judaism, and so on. The adherent of each tradition can assume that his own system of belief is the truth and that all the others are more or less true according as they approximate to it or diverge from it. Indeed this is a very natural assumption to make. And yet one only has to stand back in thought from the arena of competing systems, surveying the scene as a whole, to see something that is hidden from the Ptolemaic believer. This is the fact that the particular standpoint of a Ptolemaic theology normally depends upon where the believer happens to have been born! Having seen this, one can hardly help wondering whether it provides a sufficient basis for a conviction which involves an assessment of all other men's convictions. I myself used to hold a Ptolemaic Christian theology; but if I had been born into a devout Hindu family and had studied philosophy at, let us say, the University of Madras, I should probably have held a Ptolemaic Hindu theology instead. And if I had been born to Muslim parents, say in Egypt or Pakistan, I should probably have held a Ptolemaic Muslim theology. And so on. Having thus noted that Ptolemaic theologies tend to posit their centers on the basis of the accidents of geography, one is likely to see one's own Ptolemaic conviction in a new light. Can we be so entirely confident that to have been born in our particular part of the world carries with it the privilege of knowing the full religious truth, whereas to be born elsewhere involves the likelihood of having only partial and inferior truth?

It is not possible within the scope of such short space to go on to describe the new map of the universe of faiths which becomes visible when we make the Copernican revolution in our attitude to the religious life of mankind. Let me end by mentioning some of the questions that have to be answered by any acceptable view of the relation between Christianity and the other world faiths.

In relation to the history of religions, we have to ask how, if God has always been seeking to reveal himself to mankind, he might do this within the conditions of the world he has created. Since the early civilizations were largely separate, did they require different revelations? How would such revelations be related to the different mentalities of men in their different cultural and historical circumstances?

We have to ask: Are theologies to be regarded as divinely revealed bodies of knowledge, or as speculative human interpretations of man's religious experience? To what extent are the theologies of the different religious traditions ultimately compatible or incompatible? For example, can God be both personal and nonpersonal? Here we have to explore the possibility that the divine nature is infinite, exceeding the scope of all human concepts, and is capable of being experienced both as personal Lord and as nonpersonal ground and depth of being.

As Christians we have to do justice to our distinctive faith in the uniqueness of Christ as God the Son incarnate. Here we have to ask what sort of language this is. Does the mystery of the incarnation represent a literal or a mythological use of language? If the latter, what is the relation of the idea of incarnation to other religious mythologies? And what are the implications for Christian missions of the Copernican revolution in theology? Should mission be "sideways," into cultures dominated by other great world faiths, or "downward," into the realm of primal religion? What has been the actual pattern of missionary success in the past? What developments are likely in the "one world" so recently created by modern communications?

III
God Has Many Names

Let me first thank you for your invitation to deliver this twenty-seventh annual lecture commemorating Claude Goldsmid Montefiore. I always enjoy speaking in a synagogue and to a Jewish audience. And without being in any way an expert on Montefiore's work I have the impression—which some here will no doubt be able either to confirm or to correct—that much at least of what I am going to say would have met with his approval. In speaking of the plurality of ancient religious traditions he said (in the *Jewish Quarterly Review* of 1895), "Many pathways may all lead Godward, and the world is richer for that the paths are not new."

It is these many pathways, and the very fact of their plurality, that I want to think about with you this evening. For I wonder if you have ever considered how much simpler life would be, for everyone dealing in theology and the philosophy of religion, and indeed for every thoughtful religious believer, if there were only one religion. In a sense, from within the ongoing religious life of a particular tradition, we do in fact normally proceed as though there were only one religion, namely our own. But when we stand back from immediate involvement in the life of our own community and look

The twenty-seventh Claude Goldsmid Montefiore Lecture, delivered at the Liberal Jewish Synagogue, St. John's Wood, London, on October 16, 1980.

out beyond its borders, it is inescapably evident to us that our own religion is one of several—Buddhism, Islam, Hinduism, Judaism, Christianity, and so on. We have been like a company of people marching down a long valley, singing our own songs, developing over the centuries our own stories and slogans, unaware that over the hill there is another valley, with another great company of people marching in the same direction, but with their own language and songs and stories and ideas; and over another hill yet another marching group—each ignorant of the existence of the others. But then one day they all come out onto the same plain, the plain created by modern global communications, and see each other and wonder what to make of one another. You might think that the different groups would then simply greet one another as fellow companies of pilgrims. But in fact that is made difficult by part of the content of our respective songs and stories. For if we are Christians, we have been singing for centuries that there is no other name given among men, whereby we may be saved, than the name of Jesus. And if we are Jews, we have been singing that we are God's only chosen people, a light to lighten the world. And if we are Muslims, we have been singing that Muhammad (peace be upon him) is the seal of the prophets, bringing God's latest and final revelation. And if we are Buddhists or Hindus, we have been singing yet other songs which imply that we have the highest truth while others have only lesser and partial truths. And having thus referred to the Eastern religions, let me say that in this lecture, in which a member of one of the Semitic or Abrahamic faiths is addressing members of another faith within the same group, I am going to confine myself largely to this more restricted pluralism, with only a brief indication of the way in which my thesis applies to the great religions of the East.

Now it is of course, as we all know, entirely possible to give a naturalistic account of the whole phenomenon of religion, seeing the gods as projections of human hopes and fears. It is possible to hold that man created the gods in his own image; and that this is why different gods are worshiped in different parts of the world. Feuerbach, Marx, and Freud presented alternative versions of this thesis in its relation to Western man; and anthropologists and historians of religion have developed it on a larger scale. Whether the object of religious worship and contemplation is or is not a creation of the human imagination remains the central question for the philosophy of religion; and I have elsewhere devoted a good deal of time to the discussion of it. But if that question absorbed *all* one's time, one would never get on to any of the other important issues which also arise. And this evening I would in fact like to assume the religious interpretation of religion, as the human response to a transcendent divine Reality which is other than us, and to try from this point of view to make sense of the fact of religious pluralism. In doing so, I shall be recognizing an important element of truth in the projection theories, but shall be subsuming this truth within an account of our pluralistic human awareness of God.

In assuming the reality of the object of religious worship, religious meditation, religious experience, how are we to refer to that reality? I propose to use the term "the Eternal One." This deliberately draws upon two different sets of associations—on the one hand the ineffable One of the mystical traditions, whether it be the One of Plotinus or the One without a second of the Upanishads, and on the other hand the Holy One of theistic experience, whether it be the Holy One of Israel or of Indian theistic worship. And I am assuming, as is common ground to all the great religious traditions, that the divine reality, the Eternal One, is infinite and is in its fullness beyond the scope of human thought and language and experience; and yet that it impinges upon mankind and is encountered and conceptualized and expressed and responded to in the limited ways which are possible to our finite human nature.

Let us now bring these assumptions to the actual religious history of mankind. Men seem always to have had some dim sense of the divine, expressed in the religious practices of which there is evidence extending back half a million years or more. Indeed it is a reasonable way of defining man to stipulate that the evolving stream of hominid life had become man from the point—wherever this is to be located in the time sequence—at which a religious animal had emerged.

Our fragmentary knowledge of primitive religion is derived partly from archaeological evidence—of burial sites, showing evidence of religious symbolism in connection with death; and of sacred places, marked by stone piles, etc.—and also from the observation, particularly in the last decades of the nineteenth century, of then-surviving "primitive" tribes, mainly in Africa, Australasia and the South Sea Islands, and South America. Early man appears to have lived in very close small communities, each bound together in the kind of group mentality that prevailed prior to the emergence of self-conscious individuality. He was aware of himself as part of the social organism rather than as a separate and autonomous individual. And the group mentality was suffused by an awareness of the supernatural. Men lived in relation to an immense variety of tribal gods and spirits, in many cases personifying the forces of nature; or to ancestors and legendary figures exalted to a divine or quasi-divine status; or to the mysterious numinous power of mana in special places and people; and they were sometimes aware also of a High God, dwelling remotely in the skies, with an implicitly universal domain, though having little connection with the details of men's daily lives. The early forms of consciousness of the Eternal One seem to have been extremely dim and crude in comparison with that expressed in the teachings of any of the great spiritual masters, such as Isaiah or Jesus or Gautama or Muhammad or Kabir or Nanak. Primitive religion seems to have been a sense of an inscrutable

environing power to be feared, or of unpredictable and
often ruthless beings to be placated, an awareness which
evoked a variety of religious practices to take advantage
of their goodwill or to avoid their anger. And the moral
demand created by this primitive awareness of the Eternal One corresponded to the prevailing level of tribal
morality: a god was generally the patron of this tribe over
against that, and when the tribes went to war the gods
fought for their own, the stronger deity being assumed to
prevail. In times of danger the gods could sometimes be
propitiated with human sacrifices, so that religion had its
terrible and savage aspects, giving vent to the tribe's
fears and cruelties as well as celebrating its cohesion and
its security. Thus in the earliest stages of religious
history the Eternal One was reduced in human awareness to the dimensions of man's own image, so that the
gods were, like human kings, often cruel and bloodthirsty; or to the dimensions of the tribe or nation, as the
symbol of its unity and power; or again to the more
cosmic dimensions of the forces of nature, such as the
life-giving and yet burning radiance of the sun, or the
destructive power of storm and earthquake, or the mysterious pervasive force of fertility.

Such was the long, slow twilight of what we may call
natural religion, or religion without revelation, lasting
from the beginnings of human history down to the
spiritual dawn which occurred about three millennia
ago. We may say of that early twilight period that men
had, in virtue of the natural religious tendency of their
nature, a dim and crude sense of the Eternal One, an
awareness which took what are, from our point of view as
Jews or as Christians, at best childish and at worst
appallingly brutal and bloodthirsty forms, but which
nevertheless constituted the womb out of which the
higher religions were to be born. Here, I would say,
there was more human projection than divine disclosure.
However, the demands which the primitive consciousness of the divine made upon man's life were such as to

preserve and promote the existence of human societies, from small drifting groups to large nation-states. Religion was above all a force of social cohesion. There was at this stage no startlingly challenging impact of the Eternal One upon the human spirit, but rather that minimum presence and pressure which was to provide a basis for positive moments of revelation when mankind was ready for them. For the innumerable gods and spirits and demons were essentially projections, made possible by the innate religious character of the human mind. And yet, all this constituted the primitive response to early man's dim sense of the Eternal One. Even the cruelties of primitive religion—the sacrifices of children to appease the gods, the putting to death of chiefs when their powers waned, the slaughter of slaves to be buried with a great king, cannibalism, fearsome austerities—all these expressed, in however degraded and immature a form, men's sense of the claim of a greater reality upon their lives.

Through centuries and millennia the conditions of human life remained essentially the same, and generation after generation lived and died within this prerevelational phase of natural religion. But in the imperceptibly slow evolution of man's life through long periods of time, the conditions gradually formed for the emergence of human individuality. What these conditions were and how they developed are still largely matters of speculation. But in what Karl Jaspers has identified as the axial period or axial age, from approximately 800 to approximately 200 B.C., significant human individuals appeared through whose free responses to the Eternal One—though always within the existing setting of their own cultures—man's awareness of the divine was immensely enlarged and developed. In China, Confucius lived, and the writer or writers of the *Tao Te Ching;* and thus two great traditions, later to be labeled Confucianism and Taoism, began. In India, Gautama the Buddha, and Mahavira the founder of Jainism, both lived and taught;

and the Upanishads were produced and, at the end of this period, the *Bhagavad-Gita*. In Persia, Zoroaster transformed the existing prerevelational religion into what has been called Zoroastrianism—a religion which has since perished as an organized tradition, except for the relatively small Parsi community in India, but which nevertheless exerted a powerful influence upon developing ancient Judaism, and also through Judaism upon Christianity. In Israel, the great Hebrew prophets lived—Jeremiah, the Isaiahs, Amos, Hosea, among others. And in Greece this period produced Pythagoras, Socrates, Plato, and Aristotle. Thus the axial age was a uniquely significant band of time in man's religious history. With certain qualifications one can say that in this period all the major religious options, constituting the different forms of human awareness of the Eternal One, were identified and established, and that nothing of comparably novel significance has happened in the religious life of mankind since. To say this is of course to see Jesus and the rise of Christianity, and again Muhammad and the rise of Islam, as major new developments within the stream of Semitic monotheism that had been formed by the Hebrew prophets. Again it is to see the growth of Mahayana Buddhism (occurring at about the same time as the growth of Christianity) as a development of early Buddhism. At the other end of the axial period there are also certain qualifications to be noted. Judaism may be said to have begun, not with the work of the great prophets, but with the exodus under Moses three or four centuries before the beginning of the axial age; or indeed with the prehistoric figure of Abraham. Nevertheless, while Abraham is the semilegendary patriarch of Judaism and the exodus is its founding event, yet surely the distinctive Jewish understanding of the Eternal One and the relationship in which this understanding was embodied were formed very largely by the great prophets of the axial period. Again, in India the Vedas were written before the axial age; but, while these are foundational scriptures, the transformation of early Vedic religion into the complex of Brahmanism, the Vedanta, and Bhakti, which has constituted what has come to be called Hinduism, occurred during the axial period. Finally, there was, prior to the axial age, a brief moment of pure monotheism in Egypt under the Pharaoh Amenhotep IV; but this was quickly extinguished and left no lasting influence. There are, then, major religious events which occurred shortly before and shortly after the particularly intense concentration of such events which has come to be identified as the axial period. The concept of the axial age is thus not that of a block of time with a sharp beginning and end, nor on the other hand is it so elastic as to be stretched to include everything of significance in mankind's religious history. It is the concept of a concentration of events which, although without precise boundaries, forms a large-scale event in its own right. It differs, however, from other comparable events spread out over a number of generations in being of much wider provenance. Although the Renaissance and the Industrial Revolution, for example, have had worldwide effects, they were relatively local developments, taking place within a single civilization. But the axial period included a series of parallel movements in all the then-existing regions of relatively advanced and stable civilization. We must suppose that it was made possible by a new stage in human development, occurring at much the same time in these different ancient cultures, in which outstanding individuals emerged and were able to be channels of new religious awareness and understanding—in traditional theological terms, of divine revelation. From their work there have flowed what we know today as the great world faiths. The greatest of the spiritual movements stemming from individual founders are the nontheistic religions of Buddhism and Confucianism and the theistic religions of Christianity and Islam. Each of these arose out of a prior tradition of immemorial antiquity—Buddhism coming out of the Hindu stream of religious life;

Confucianism (and also Taoism) from the existing Chinese tradition; Christianity out of Jewish religious life; and Islam, though less directly, out of the Judeo-Christian tradition. Alongside these there also flows the "primal" religious life of Africa as, arguably, another major world faith.

Let us then think of the Eternal One as pressing in upon the human spirit, seeking to be known and responded to by man, and seeking through man's free responses to create the human animal into (in our Judeo-Christian language) a child of God, or toward a perfected humanity. And let us suppose that in that first millennium B.C. human life had developed to the point at which man was able to receive and respond to a new and much fuller vision of the divine reality and of the claim of that reality upon his life. Such a breakthrough is traditionally called revelation, and the revelation was, as I have pointed out, already plural. But should we not expect there to have been *one* single revelation for all mankind, rather than several different revelations? The answer, I suggest, is no—not if we take seriously into account the actual facts of human life in history. For in that distant period, some two and a half thousand years ago, the civilizations of China, of India, and of the Near East could almost have been located on different planets, so tenuous and slow were the lines of communication between them. A divine revelation intended for all mankind but occurring in China, or in India, or in Israel would have taken many centuries to spread to the other countries. But we are supposing that the source of revelation was always seeking to communicate to mankind, and in new ways to as much of mankind as was living within the higher civilizations that had then developed. From this point of view it seems natural that the revelation should have been plural, occurring separately in the different centers of human culture.

But now let me turn to the epistemology of revelation. Thomas Aquinas stated a profound epistemological truth,

which has an even wider application than he realized,
when he said that "The thing known is in the knower
according to the mode of the knower" (*Summa Theologica*, II/II, Q.1, art. 2). In other words, our awareness of
something is the awareness that we are able to have,
given our own particular nature and the particular character of our cognitive machinery. This is true of all types
of knowledge—sense perception, moral awareness, and
religious awareness. In relation to the physical environment, our cognitive machinery, consisting in our sense
organs and neurosystem, together with the selecting and
organizing function of the mind/brain, has a twofold
function: to make us aware of certain aspects of our
environment and at the same time to preserve us from
being aware of other aspects of it. We are aware of our
physical environment, not as it is in itself, in its virtually
infinite complexity, but as it appears to creatures with
our particular cognitive machinery. Other forms of animal life presumably experience the same world differently, each in its own way. The point I am making here is
that in ordinary sense perception "the thing known" is
known "according to the mode of the knower." At this
physical level, however, the "mode of the knower" is
only to a very slight extent under the control of the
knower. We are genetically programmed to experience
as we do. For we are all compelled, ultimately on pain of
death, to experience the world as it actually is in its
relationship to us. Our cognitive freedom is at a minimum at this level.

At the level of moral awareness, however, we have a
much greater degree of cognitive freedom, and the correlative of this freedom is responsibility. If we do not
want to be conscious of a moral obligation, we are able to
rethink the situation and so come to see it in a different
light. This is the way in which human wickedness
normally operates, namely by self-deception. We do not
say to ourselves: This is clearly wrong, but I shall do it
nevertheless. We say: Given all the circumstances, this is

the necessary and therefore the right thing to do. And this capacity to deceive ourselves is an aspect of our moral freedom. If we were not capable of such subtle self-deception, we would perhaps be more admirable creatures, but on the other hand we would not be the morally free and responsible creatures that we are.

When we now turn to religious awareness we find a yet greater and more crucial degree of cognitive freedom and responsibility, without which we should not be personal beings, capable of a free response to the Eternal One. Let me put the point in explicitly theistic terms. We can imagine finite personal beings created in the immediate presence of God, so that in being conscious of that which is other than themselves they are automatically and unavoidably conscious of God. They are conscious of existing in the presence and under the all-seeing gaze of infinite being, infinite power, infinite wisdom and goodness and love. But how, in that situation, could they have any genuine freedom in relation to their creator? In order to have such freedom must they not exist at a certain distance from him? And so, in creating finite personal life, God has created the space-time universe as a system which functions in accordance with its own inner laws. And man has been produced within and as part of this universe. Because the universe has its own autonomy it is religiously ambiguous—capable of being experienced both religiously and nonreligiously. What we call faith is the interpretative element in the religious way of experiencing the world and our lives within it. And faith is an act of cognitive freedom and responsibility. It reflects the extent to which we are willing, and ready, to exist consciously in the presence of the infinite reality in which being and value are one. In other words, the thing known—namely the Eternal One—is known according to the mode of the knower; and at this level the cognitive mode of the knower is largely under the knower's own control. He is able to shut out what he does not want, or is not ready, to let in. And so it is that within each of the great streams of religious experience and thought—Judaism and Christianity being two such streams—there are enormous individual variations in the degree of personal response and commitment. There are practicing and nonpracticing, real and nominal, saintly and very unsaintly Jews and Christians.

But I want now to extend the principle that the thing known is known according to the mode of the knower, in order to throw light upon the fact of religious pluralism.

And so we come back to our original question, Why should religious faith take a number of such different forms? Because, I would suggest, religious faith is not an isolated aspect of our lives but is closely bound up with human culture and human history, which are in turn bound up with basic geographical, climatic, and economic circumstances. It has been pointed out, for example, that "in nomadic, pastoral, herd-keeping societies the male principle predominates; whereas among agricultural peoples, aware of the fertile earth which brings forth from itself and nourishes its progeny upon its broad bosom, it is the mother-principle which seems important. . . . Among Semitic peoples therefore, whose traditions are those of herdsmen, the sacred is thought of in male terms: God the father. Among Indian peoples whose tradition has been for many centuries, and even millennia, agricultural, it is in female terms that the sacred is understood: God the mother." (Trevor Ling, *A History of Religion, East and West*, p. 146; London: Macmillan & Co., 1968). Again, as has been pointed out by Martin Prozesky, the Canaanites, and other ancient Near Eastern cultures with a comparable mythology, worshiped a sky god (Baal) and an earth goddess (Anath), whereas the ancient Egyptians, in contrast, had a sky goddess (Nut) and an earth god (Geb). Why was Egypt different in this respect? Is it not because Egypt is in the exceptional position that the fertilizing waters, male by analogy, come from the earth, in the form of the river Nile, whereas in the other countries they come from the sky in the form of rain? Now one could, as I mentioned earlier, react to this kind of evidence by concluding that the belief in God is entirely a human projection, guided by cultural influences. But the alternative interpretation is that there is some genuine awareness of the divine, but that the concrete form which it takes is provided by cultural factors. On this view these different human awarenesses of the Eternal One represent different culturally conditioned perceptions of the same infinite divine reality.

To develop this hypothesis, we must, I think, distinguish between the Eternal One in itself, in its eternal self-existent being, beyond relationship to a creation, and the Eternal One in relation to mankind and as perceived from within our different human cultural situations. Man's awareness of the Eternal One—like all our awareness of reality—is focused by concepts. There are in fact two different basic concepts involved in the religious life of mankind. One is the concept of deity, or of the Eternal One as personal, which presides over the theistic modes of religion; and the other is the concept of the Absolute, or of the Eternal One as nonpersonal, which presides over the nontheistic or transtheistic modes of religion. We only have time to be concerned about the theistic modes here. The concept of deity, or of God, takes concrete form, and a "local habitation and a name," in the life of a particular human community and culture as a specific divine *persona* or face or image or icon of the Eternal One. Yahweh of Israel is one such divine *persona*. He exists in relationship with the people of Israel, and cannot be characterized except in that relationship. He has to be described historically as the God of Abraham, of Isaac, and of Jacob, who brought the children of Israel out of bondage in Egypt and led them into their Promised Land. You cannot abstract Yahweh from his historical relationship with this particular people. He is a part of their history and they are a part of his. He is, according to my hypothesis, the divine *persona* in relation to the Jewish people. And as such he represents a genuine, authentic, valid human perception of the Eternal One from within a particular human culture and strand of history. But he is a different divine *persona* from, say, Shiva or from Krishna, who are divine *personae* in relation respectively to the Shaivite and the Vaishnavite communities of India. Thus the many gods are not separate and distinct divine beings, but rather different *personae* formed in the interaction of divine presence and human projection. The divine presence is the presence of the Eternal One to our finite human consciousness, and the human projections are the culturally conditioned images and symbols in terms of which we concretize the basic concept of deity.

Summarizing this hypothesis in philosophical terms made possible by the work of Immanuel Kant, we may distinguish between, on the one hand, the single divine noumenon, the Eternal One in itself, transcending the scope of human thought and language, and, on the other hand, the plurality of divine phenomena, the divine *personae* of the theistic religions and the concretizations of the concept of the Absolute in the nontheistic religions. Among the former are Yahweh (or Adonai), and Allah, and the God and Father of Jesus Christ, and Krishna, and Shiva, and many, many more. The principal instances of the latter—the nonpersonal awareness of the Eternal One—are the Brahman of advaitic Hinduism, the Nirvana of Theravada Buddhism, and the Sunyata of Mahayana Buddhism. And each of these forms in which the Eternal One has been perceived by human beings is integral to a complex totality which constitutes what we call a religion, with its distinctive forms of religious experience, its own myths and symbols, its theological systems, its liturgies and its art, its ethics and life-styles, its scriptures and traditions—these elements all interacting with and reinforcing one another. And these different totalities constitute varying human responses, within the setting of the different cultures or forms of human life, to the same infinite transcendent divine reality, which we are calling the Eternal One.

Now, finally, let us return to the exclusive claims which each of the great world faiths has developed in the course of its history. Each is accustomed to think of itself as in some important sense superior to all the others; and this thought has usually become welded into its belief system and expressed in its scriptures and liturgies. Is it possible, however, to stand outside these different traditions and to judge their respective merits, and perhaps to conclude that one is in fact superior to the others? Such a judgment might be attempted on either moral or spiritual grounds.

At this point a very important caution is to be observed. Although I have spoken of the different religions as totalities, it has to be added that they are complex, polymorphous, and ever-changing totalities. Thus, for example, Christianity, if we take its entire range throughout its long history, includes many contradictory elements: not only a strong emphasis upon the personal character of God but also a persistent strand of theological and mystical thought in which God is characterized as pure being, or being-itself, or the ground of being, or the depth of being, etc.; again, not only its world-affirming materialism but also its world-denying ascetic, contemplative, and monastic strands; not only, today, pride in modern science as supposedly its own offspring but also earlier vigorous attempts to strangle modern science at birth; not only teaching of unsurpassed power about love of neighbor, and even of enemy, and about forgiveness and peace, but also a long history of persecution and conflict, violence and bloodshed, so that there has been no war involving a Christian nation which has not been supported and blessed by the churches. And each of the other great world religions appears as equally internally complex and multiform and even self-contradictory when we see it spread out along the axis of history. Each has had its periods of spiritual flourishing, its great moments of renewal and reform, its times of cultural creativity and flowering, but also its dark ages, its chauvinistic and regressive moods, and most have had their fits of blind hatred and savage violence. Again, each has produced comparable saints and prophets and thinkers, but also comparable scoundrels and hypocrites and despots and oppressors. Thus the religious totalities are each so complex and various that it is very hard, if not impossible, to make global moral judgments about them. Given a presupposed set of moral criteria, one can point to elements in Christian, or Muslim, or Jewish, or Buddhist history and culture which are admirable and to other elements which are reprehensible. But to weigh all these up together in a common scale and reach an overall moral appraisal is probably impossible. Further, there is the problem that the presupposed set of moral criteria with which one operates will be those of one's own tradition, so that there enters in the whole question, of which we are increasingly conscious today, of the relativity of moral ideas to different cultural and historical circumstances. I really think, therefore, that the project of a comparative ethical assessment of the great religious totalities leads into an impossible morass from which nothing useful can emerge.

But if comparative moral judgments about such vast and complex slices of the human story are impossibly difficult to make, what about purely religious and spiritual comparisons? Can we not say, for example, that the awareness of the Eternal One as a personal God is spiritually superior to the awareness of the Eternal One as the Brahman of Hinduism? We can say this, in the sense that many Christians and Jews and Muslims do; but on the other hand many Hindus of the advaitic tradition say the contrary, namely, that the awareness of Brahman as a divine person represents a spiritually lower and cruder form of awareness. How can we hope to resolve such a dispute? We cannot, except simply by confessional assertion. But perhaps we would do better to question the underlying assumption that one major human response to the Eternal One has to be superior, as a totality, to all others. Why must this be so? May it not rather be that there are several *different* forms of human awareness of and response to the Eternal One, which are each valid and effective in spite of being different? Should we not perhaps reject the assumption of one and only one true religion in favor of the alternative possibility of a genuine religious pluralism?

Let me emphasize at this point that I have been speaking of what we commonly call the great world faiths, not of primitive religion, not of religious movements which have perished, and not of the many new religious movements which are springing up around us all the time. There is a law of the survival of the spiritually fittest which simplifies the religious scene. But when we are confronted by a stream of religious life and thought and experience that has persisted for many centuries, which has produced inspiring scriptures and a rich succession of saints and prophets and profound thinkers, and has provided a spiritual home in which hundreds of millions of human lives have been lived, then I think we have to assume that it represents a genuine awareness of and response to the Eternal One. And I do not believe that we have any objective grounds on which to claim that our own slice of history and tradition is better as a totality than another of the ancient and great traditions. Subjectively, however, each tradition is unique and superior for those who have been spiritually formed by it. For a religion produces in those who have been born and brought up within it souls adapted to that religion, who would accordingly not be at home in any other. It is only when a stream of religious life begins to lose its vitality that some of its population lapse into merely nominal adherence or are attracted away to a different faith. And this is of course the religious situation throughout much of our modern industrialized Western world. But even here the particular religious culture in which we have been formed still has a strong hold. For most Christians in this country Christianity is the religion to which they adhere or against which they rebel; and they are so deeply formed by this tradition, in ways of which they are perhaps often hardly conscious, that not many could become, say, Muslims or Buddhists. Again, not many Muslims or Buddhists could become Christians or Hindus. And I presume that a Jew can hardly imagine not being a Jew, however far he may lapse from Jewish observances. It was a rabbi who said, "Many Jews today do not believe in God, but they nearly all believe that God believes in them!" And, in short, we are so formed by the tradition into which we were born and in which we were raised that it is for us unique and absolute and final. Yet I believe that when we accept the fact of religious pluralism we have to learn to refrain from converting that psychological absoluteness into a claim to the objective absoluteness and superiority of our own faith in comparison with all others.

But to refrain from absolute and exclusive claims is harder for some traditions than for others. For the great business of religion is salvation, the bringing of men and women to fullness of life or perfection of being in relation to the Eternal One. And so religious absolutism takes the form of a claim to be the sole way of salvation. It is not, I would think, too difficult for Judaism to avoid making such a claim. The key concept here is that of God's Chosen People. But this need not mean, and has indeed perhaps never meant, that there is salvation only for Jews. Rather it represents the awareness of a divine vocation to bear witness to God for the good of all mankind. But such an awareness is presumably compatible with others having their own religious vocations. Indeed, every encounter with the Eternal One, when it takes a theistic form, involves a sense of being specifically called, and thus chosen. We are all, I would say, chosen people, though chosen in different ways and for different vocations.

But it is much harder for Christianity to digest the fact of religious pluralism. Here the key concept is that of divine incarnation. There is a direct line of logical entailment from the premise that Jesus was God, in the sense that he was God the Son, the second Person of a divine Trinity, living a human life, to the conclusion that Christianity, and Christianity alone, was founded by God in person; and from this to the further conclusion that God must want all his human children to be related to him through this religion which he has himself founded for us; and then to the final conclusion, drawn in the Roman Catholic dogma "Outside the church, no salvation" and its Protestant missionary equivalent "Outside Christianity, no salvation." Today, increasing numbers of Christians find that conclusion unacceptable, because untrue to the evident religious facts. We have, then, to work back up the chain of inference and eventually to question the original premise. This has indeed in any case to be reconsidered in the light of the conclusion of so much modern biblical scholarship that the historical Jesus very probably did not claim to be God, or to be God the Son, the second Person of a Trinity, incarnate. The conclusion to which some of us within the Christian fold have come is that the idea of divine incarnation is a metaphorical (or, in technical theological language, a mythological) rather than a literal idea. Incarnation, in the sense of the embodiment of ideas, values, insights in human living, is a basic metaphor. One might say, for example, that in 1940 the spirit of defiance of the British people against Nazi Germany was incarnated in Winston Churchill. Now we want to say of Jesus that he was so vividly conscious of God as the loving heavenly Father, and so startlingly open to God and so fully his servant and instrument, that the divine love was expressed, and in that sense incarnated, in his life. This was not a matter (as it is in official Christian doctrine) of Jesus having two complete natures, one human and the other divine. He was wholly human; but whenever self-giving love in response to the love of God is lived out in a human life, to that extent the divine love has become incarnate on earth. Some such reinterpretation of the idea of incarnation appeals to a number of Christians today, while on the other hand it is resisted by many more; and one cannot at present foresee how this internal Christian debate will eventually go.

But I must be drawing to an end. When I say in a summarizing slogan that God has many names, I mean that the Eternal One is perceived within different human cultures under different forms, both personal and nonpersonal, and that from these different perceptions arise the religious ways of life which we call the great world faiths. The practical upshot of this thesis is that people of the different religious traditions are free to see one another as friends rather than as enemies or rivals. We are members of different households of faith, but households each of which has some precious and distinctive contact with the Eternal One, which others can perhaps learn to share. We should, then, go forward into the new age of growing interreligious dialogue with hope and with positive anticipations and with a sense of pleasurable excitement.

IV
"By Whatever Path . . ."

For many of us in the West the relation between Christianity and the other world religions has until recently been a rather theoretical issue to which rather theoretical responses have seemed sufficient. We have lived within the cultural borders of Christendom and—many of us—within the ecclesiastical borders of the church. From this center we—that is, our forebears, and still the church today—have been sending out missionaries into all the continents of the earth and have enjoyed a vague sense that the world is, however tardily, in process of becoming Christianized. And so we have in the past generally thought of the non-Christian world in negative terms, as the unfortunate not-yet-Christianized portion of humanity and as potential recipients of the divine grace which is coming through the missionaries whom we send out to them.

However, several things have happened to shatter this attitude of religious imperialism.

One has been the growing awareness, produced by the news media and by travel, of the sheer size and religious variety of mankind outside our own Anglo-Saxon tribe. The estimated Christian population of the world is 983.6 million, constituting just under a quarter of the world's total population of 4,123.9 million (*Encyclopaedia Britannica 1978 Book of the Year*, p. 616). But while the total number of Christians is slowly rising, the proportion of Christians is slowly declining, because the explosion in the human population (the number of which will have roughly doubled between 1970 and about 2005) is taking place more rapidly outside Christendom than within it. Thus the Christian faith is held today, as in the past, only by a minority of the human race; and it looks as though this minority may well be smaller rather than larger in the future. This thought casts a massive shadow over any assumption that it is God's will that all mankind shall be converted to Christianity.

Again, it is a fact evident to ordinary people (even though not always taken into account by theologians) that in the great majority of cases—say 98 or 99 percent—the religion in which a person believes and to which he adheres depends upon where he was born. That is to say, if someone is born to Muslim parents in Egypt or Pakistan, that person is very likely to be a Muslim; if to Buddhist parents in Sri Lanka or Burma, that person is very likely to be a Buddhist; if to Hindu parents in India, that person is very likely to be a Hindu; if to Christian parents in Europe or the Americas, that person is very likely to be a Christian. Of course in each case he may be a fully committed or a merely nominal adherent of his religion. But whether one is a Christian, a Jew, a Muslim, a Buddhist, a Sikh, a Hindu—or for that matter a Marxist or a Maoist—depends nearly always on the part of the world in which one happens to have been born. Any credible religious faith must be able to make sense of this circumstance. And a credible Christian faith must make sense of it by relating it to the universal sovereignty and fatherhood of God. This is rather conspicuously not done by the older theology which held that God's saving activity is confined within a single narrow thread of human life, namely that recorded in our own scriptures.

Another factor making for change is that the old unflattering caricatures of other religions are now being replaced by knowledge based on serious objective study. Our bookshops now carry shelves of good popular as well as technical works on the history of religion, the phenomenology of religion, and the comparative study of religions; and only one who prefers to be ignorant can any longer complacently congratulate himself upon knowing nothing about other faiths. It is no longer acceptable to plead ignorance concerning the wider religious life of mankind as an excuse for parochial theological prejudices. Times have changed and today no one wishes to present the eighteenth-century image of Fielding's Parson Thwackum who said: "When I mention religion, I mean the Christian religion; and not only the Christian religion, but the Protestant religion; and not only the Protestant religion, but the Church of England."

And, for those living in Britain, since the 1950s Asian immigration from India, Pakistan, and (as it now is) Bangladesh has brought sizable Muslim, Hindu, and Sikh communities to many of our cities, adding three more non-Christian groups to the Jews who had already been there for more than two centuries. By their very existence these non-Christian communities have presented the church with a number of new questions, which it has generally chosen to see as difficult problems. Should we try to help the Muslims, Sikhs, and Hindus to find suitable premises in which to worship? Should we be willing to sell them redundant church buildings? Should local religious broadcasting include or exclude them? Should we try to insist that all children in the state schools shall receive Christian religious instruction, regardless of the religion which they or their parents profess? And so on. These questions all have theological implications and have helped to turn the attention of Christians to the problem of the relation of Christianity to the other world religions.

I

When you visit the various non-Christian places of worship in one of our big cities you discover—possibly with a shock of surprise—that phenomenologically (or in other words, to human observation) the same kind of thing is taking place in them as in a Christian church. That is to say, human beings are coming together to open their minds to a higher reality, which is thought of as the personal creator and Lord of the universe, and as making vital moral demands upon the lives of men and women. Of course the trappings are very different—in a church men wear shoes and no hat; in mosque, gurdwara, and temple, a hat and no shoes; in a synagogue both. In some you sit on a pew, in others on the floor. In some there is singing, in others there is not. Different musical instruments or none are used. More important, the supreme being is referred to as God in a Christian church, as Adonai in a Jewish synagogue, as Allah in a Muslim mosque, as Ekoamkar in a Sikh gurdwara, as Rama or as Krishna in a Hindu temple. And yet there is an important sense in which what is being done in the several forms of worship is essentially the same.

In the Jewish synagogue God is worshiped as maker of heaven and earth, and as the God of Abraham and Isaac and Jacob, who led the children of Israel out of Egypt into the Promised Land and who has called them to live as a light to lighten the world. Worship is very close in form and ethos to Christian worship in the Protestant traditions. Here is a passage of typical Jewish prayer: "With a great love have You loved us, O Lord our God, and with exceeding compassion have You pitied us. Our Father and King, our fathers trusted in You, and You taught them the laws of life: be gracious also to us, and teach us. Have compassion upon us, and guide us, our Merciful Father, that we may grasp and understand, learn and teach, observe and uphold with love all the words of Your law." (From the Weekday Morning Service in *Service of the Heart: Weekday Sabbath and Festival Services and Prayers for Home and Synagogue*, pp. 40f.; London: Union of Liberal and Progressive Synagogues, 1967.)

In Muslim mosques God is worshiped as the maker of heaven and earth, and as the sovereign Lord of the universe, omnipotent, holy, and merciful, before whom men bow in absolute submission. Here is a typical passage of Muslim prayer: "Praise be to God, Lord of creation, Source of all livelihood, who orders the morning, Lord of majesty and honour, of grace and beneficence. He who is so far that he may not be seen and so near that he witnesses the secret things. Blessed be he and for ever exalted." (Kenneth Cragg, ed., *Alive to God: Muslim and Christian Prayer*, p. 65; London: Oxford University Press, 1970.) Or again: "To God belongs the praise, Lord of the heavens and Lord of the earth, the Lord of all being. His is the dominion in the heavens and in the earth: he is the Almighty, the All-wise" (*Alive to God*, p. 61).

In Sikh gurdwaras God is worshiped as the maker of heaven and earth, the gracious Lord of time and of eternity, who demands righteousness and seeks peace and goodwill between men. Here is part of the Sikh morning prayer:

> There is but one God.
> He is all that is.
> He is the Creator of all things
> and He is all-pervasive.
> He is without fear
> and without enmity.
> He is timeless and unborn
> and self-existent.
> He is the Enlightener
> And can be realized by grace
> of Himself alone.
> He was in the beginning;
> He was in all ages.
> The True One is and was
> and shall forever be.

(Japji)

The Hindu temples which have been established in Britain represent the Bhakti or theistic-devotional form of Hinduism. In them God is worshiped as the ultimate Lord of all, the infinite divine Life known under many aspects and names. Against the background of throbbing music the name of God is chanted again and again by ecstatic worshipers. The language of Bhakti devotion is emotional and personal. Here is a typical hymn:

> O save me, save me, Mightiest,
> Save me and set me free.
> O let the love that fills my breast
> Cling to thee lovingly.
>
> Grant me to taste how sweet thou art;
> Grant me but this, I pray,
> And never shall my love depart
> Or turn from thee away.
>
> Then I thy name shall magnify
> And tell thy praise abroad,
> For very love and gladness I
> Shall dance before my God.
>
> (A. C. Bouquet, ed.,
> *Sacred Books of the World*,
> p. 246; Pelican Books, 1954)

And here is another Bhakti devotional hymn:

> Now all my days with joy I'll fill, full to
> the brim,
> With all my heart to Vitthal cling, and
> only Him.
>
> He will sweep utterly away all dole
> and care;
> And all in sunder shall I rend illusion's
> snare.
>
> O altogether dear is He, and He alone,
> For all my burden He will take to be
> His own.

Lo, all the sorrow of the world will
straightway cease,
And all unending now shall be the
reign of peace.

(*Sacred Books of the World*, p. 245)

II

In the light of the phenomenological similarity of
worship in these different traditions we have to ask
whether people in church, synagogue, mosque, gurdwara, and temple are worshiping different Gods or are
worshiping the same God? Are Adonai and God, Allah
and Ekoamkar, Rama and Krishna different gods, or are
these different names for the same ultimate Being?
There would seem to be three possibilities. One is that
there exist, ontologically, many gods. But this conflicts
with the belief concerning each that he is the creator
source of the world. A second possibility is that one faith-
community, let us say our own, worships God while the
others vainly worship images which exist only in their
imaginations. But even within Christianity itself, is there
not a variety of overlapping mental images of God—for
example, as stern judge and predestinating power, and as
gracious and loving heavenly Father—so that different
Christian groups, and even different Christian individuals, are worshiping the divine Being through their
different images of him? And do not the glimpses which I
have just offered of worship within the various religious
traditions suggest that our Christian images overlap with
many non-Christian images of God? If so, a third possibility must seem the most probable, namely, that there is
but one God, who is maker and lord of all; that in his
infinite fullness and richness of being he exceeds all our
human attempts to grasp him in thought; and that the
devout in the various great world religions are in fact

worshiping that one God, but through different, overlapping concepts or mental icons of him.

If this is so, the older Christian view of other faiths as areas of spiritual darkness within which there is no salvation, no knowledge of God, and no acceptable worship must be mistaken. We need instead, I believe, an epistemology of religion of the kind that will be suggested in Chapters V and VI. To offer a preliminary glimpse of this now, it hinges upon the Kantian distinction between reality as it is in itself and that same reality as it is experienced by human beings. In all our conscious experiencing of our environment the perceiving mind is itself active, both selecting and integrating in terms of concepts and schema; so that the world as experienced is inevitably less and other than the world as it is in itself. The same basic pattern applies, I suggest, to our human experience of the divine. We are not directly aware of the divine reality as it is in itself, but only as experienced from our distinctively human point of view. This is inevitably a partial awareness, limited by our human finitude and imperfections. We "see through a glass, darkly"; and the glass is constituted by the set of human concepts operating within our cultures. The result is the range of ways of conceiving and experiencing the divine that is to be found within the history of religions.

The older Christian view of other faiths has come to seem increasingly implausible and unrealistic in the light of growing knowledge of other faiths and as a result of better contacts with their adherents. Consequently Christian theologians, perhaps most notably within the Roman communion, have been making strenuous efforts to escape from the unacceptable implications of the older view, though usually without feeling entitled explicitly to renounce it. This is, of course, in accordance with the established ecclesiastical method of developing and changing doctrine. One cannot say that a formerly proclaimed dogma was wrong, but one can reinterpret it to

mean something very different from what it was originally understood to mean. Such exercises often display a
high level of ingenuity, though no amount of intellectual
sophistication can save them from seeming slightly ridic-
ulous or slightly dishonest to the outsider. At any rate, in
the attempt to retain the dogma of no salvation outside
the church, or outside Christianity, we have the ideas of
implicit, as distinguished from explicit, faith; of baptism
by desire, as distinguished from literal baptism; and, as a
Protestant equivalent, the idea of the latent church as
distinguished from the manifest church; and, again, the
suggestion that men can only come to God through Jesus
Christ, but that those who have not encountered him in
this life will encounter him in the life to come. Or again
there is Karl Rahner's notion of the anonymous Christian
(*Theological Investigations*, Vol. 5, 1966, Ch. 6; Rahner's
most recent discussion, reaffirming the notion, occurs in
Theological Investigations, Vol. 14, 1976, Ch. 17; see
also Vol. 16, 1979, Ch. 13). The devout Muslim, or
Hindu, or Sikh, or Jew can be regarded as an anonymous
Christian, this being an honorary status granted unilater-
ally to people who have not expressed any desire for it.
Or again there is the claim that Christianity, properly
understood, is not a religion but is a revelation which
judges and supersedes all religions. Or finally there is
Hans Küng's distinction between the ordinary way of
salvation in the world religions and the extraordinary
way in the church. Küng says: "A man is to be saved
within the religion that is made available to him in his
historical situation. Hence it is his right and his duty to
seek God within that religion in which the hidden God
has already found him." Thus the world religions are, he
says, "the way of salvation in universal salvation history;
the general way of salvation, we can even say, for the
people of the world religions: the more common, the
'ordinary' way of salvation, as against which the way of
salvation in the Church appears as something very special and extraordinary" (in Neuner, ed., *Christian Reve-*

lation and World Religions, pp. 52f.). This sounds at first extremely promising. However, Küng goes on to take away with one hand what he has given with the other. The ordinary way of salvation for the majority of mankind in the world religions turns out to be only an interim way until, sooner or later, they come to an explicit Christian faith. The people of the world religions are, he says, "pre-Christian, directed towards Christ. ... The men of the world religions are not professing Christians but, by the grace of God, they are called and marked out to be Christians" (Neuner, pp. 55f.). (For Küng's more recent views, see his *On Being a Christian,* A III; Doubleday & Co., 1976.) One is reminded of the British amnesty for illegal immigrants. Although they are unauthorized entrants into the Kingdom of Heaven, the Indian and Pakistani and other foreign worshipers of God will be accepted if sooner or later they come forward to be legally registered by Christian baptism!

III

Thus all of these thinkers, who are trying so hard to find room for their non-Christian brethren in the sphere of salvation, are still working within the presuppositions of the old dogma. Only Christians can be saved; so we have to say that devout and godly non-Christians are really, in some metaphysical sense, Christians or Christians-to-be without knowing it. Although to the ordinary nonecclesiastical mind this borders upon doubletalk, in intention it is a charitable extension of the sphere of grace to people who had formerly been regarded as beyond the pale. As such it can function as a psychological bridge between the no-longer-acceptable older view and the new view which is emerging. But sooner or later we have to get off the bridge on to the other side. We have to make what might be called a Copernican revolution in our theology of religions. You will remember from our discussion in Chapter II that the old Ptolemaic astronomy held that the earth is the center of the solar system and that all the other heavenly bodies revolve around it. And when it was realized that this theory did not fit the observed facts, particularly the wandering movements of the planets, epicycles were added, circles revolving on circles, to complicate the theory and bring it nearer to the facts. By analogy the "no salvation outside Christianity" doctrine is theologically Ptolemaic. Christianity is seen as the center of the universe of faiths, and all the other religions are regarded as revolving around it and as being graded in value according to their distance from it. And the theories of implicit faith, baptism by desire, anonymous Christianity, the latent church, the "ordinary" and "extraordinary" ways of salvation, and the claim that the Christian religion is not a religion whereas all the others are, are so many epicycles added to this Ptolemaic theology to try to accommodate our growing knowledge of other faiths and our awareness of the true piety and devotion which they sustain.

It is also worth repeating that just as a Ptolemaic astronomy could be developed, not only from the standpoint of this earth, but from any of the other planets, so also a Ptolemaic theology can be developed not only from a Christian standpoint but equally from the standpoint of any other faith. From, let us say, a Hindu center one could say that devout Christians are implicit Hindus by virtue of their sincere desire for the truth even though they do not yet know what the truth is; that other faiths provide the "ordinary" way of salvation while Hinduism is the "extraordinary" way, in which the truth is manifest which in the others is latent; that Hinduism is not a religion but the eternal truth judging and superseding all religions. The Ptolemaic stance can be taken by anyone. But it can only serve as an interim position while we prepare our minds for a Copernican revolution. Copernicus realized that it is the sun, and not the earth, that is at the center, and that all the heavenly bodies, including our own earth, revolve around it. And we have to realize that the universe of faiths centers upon *God*, and not upon Christianity or upon any other religion. He is the sun, the originative source of light and life, whom all the religions reflect in their own different ways. This must mean that the different world religions have each served as God's means of revelation to a different stream of human life. Such a conclusion makes sense of the history of religions. The first period was one in which the innate religiousness of the human mind expressed itself in the different forms of what we can call natural religion—the worship of spirits, ancestors, nature gods, and often bloodthirsty national deities. But—as we noted in Chapter III—about 800 B.C. there began what Karl Jaspers (*The Origin and Goal of History;* Yale University Press, 1953) has called the axial period, in which seminal moments of religious experience occurred in each of the four principal centers of civilization—Greece, the Near East, India, and China—out of which the higher religions have come. In this immensely rich and important band of time the great Hebrew prophets lived; in Persia, Zoroaster; in China, Confucius and the author (or authors) of the Taoist scriptures; in India, the Buddha, and Mahavira, and the writers of the Upanishads and later of the *Bhagavad-Gita;* in Greece, Pythagoras, Socrates, and Plato. And then later, out of the stream of prophetic religion established by the Hebrew prophets there came Jesus and the rise of Christianity, and Muhammad and the rise of Islam.

Now in this axial period, during the first millennium B.C., communication between the continents and civilizations of the earth was so slow that for all practical purposes men lived in different cultural worlds. There could not be a divine revelation, through any human means, to mankind as a whole, but only separate revelations within the different streams of human history. And so it is a natural and indeed an inevitable hypothesis that God, the ultimate divine reality, was in this axial period becoming known to mankind through a number of specially sensitive and responsive spirits. In each case the revelatory experiences, and the religious traditions to which they gave rise, were conditioned by the history, culture, language, climate, and indeed all the concrete circumstances of human life at that particular time and place. Thus the cultural and philosophical form of the revelation of the divine is characteristically different in each case, although we may believe that everywhere the one Spirit has been at work, pressing in upon the human spirit.

IV

I shall return presently to this historical view of the different religious traditions to ask what difference it makes that the world has now become a communicational unity. But let me first ask the question that is so important to us as Christians, namely, what does all this imply concerning the person of our Lord? What about the uniqueness of Christ, the belief that Jesus was God incarnate, the second Person of the holy Trinity become man, the eternal Logos made flesh? Did he not say, "I and the Father are one," and "No one comes to the Father, but by me"? Here, unfortunately, we have to enter the realm of New Testament criticism: and I say "unfortunately" because of the notorious uncertainties of this realm. There are powerful schools of thought, following fashions which tend to change from generation to generation, but no consensus either across the years or across the schools. But this at least can be said: that whereas until some three or four generations ago it was generally accepted among biblical scholars that Jesus claimed to be God the Son, with a unique consciousness of divinity, so that the doctrine of the incarnation was believed to be firmly based in the consciousness and teaching of Jesus himself, today this is no longer generally held and is indeed very widely thought not to be the case. I am not going to enter into a detailed discussion of the New Testament evidence: I am neither competent to do this, nor is there space. I will only quote some summarizing words of Wolfhart Pannenberg in his massive work *Jesus—God and Man* (Westminster Press, 1968), where he says: "After D. F. Strauss and F. C. Bauer, John's Gospel could not longer be claimed uncritically as a historical source of authentic words of Jesus. Consequently, other concepts and titles that were more indirectly connected with Jesus' relation to God came into the foreground of the question of Jesus' 'Messianic self-consciousness.' However, the transfer of these titles to Jesus . . . has been demonstrated with growing certainty by critical study of the Gospels to be the work of the post-Easter community. Today it must be taken as all but certain that the pre-Easter Jesus neither designated himself as Messiah (or Son of God) nor accepted such a confession to him from others" (p. 237). Not all New Testament scholars would endorse Pannenberg's words. But certainly one can no longer regard it as a fact proved out of the New Testament that Jesus thought of himself as God incarnate. On the contrary, this now seems to be very unlikely. And certainly we cannot rest anything on the assumption that the great Christological sayings of the Fourth Gospel (such as "I and my Father are one") were ever spoken, in sober historical fact, by the Jesus who walked the hills and villages of Galilee. It seems altogether more probable that they reflect the developing theology of the church toward the end of the first century.

Now if Jesus himself did not think of himself as God incarnate, one might well ask whether his disciples ought to do so. But instead of pursuing that question directly, it seems more profitable to accept that the Son-of-God and God-incarnate language has become deeply entrenched in the discourse of Christian thought and piety, and to ask what *kind* of language it is. Is the statement that Jesus was God incarnate, or the Son of God, or God the Son, a statement of literal fact; and if so, what precisely is the fact? Or is it a poetic, or symbolic, or mythological statement? It can, I think, only be the latter. It can hardly be a literal, factual statement, since after nearly two thousand years of Christian reflection no factual content has been discerned in it—unless, that is, we give it factual content in terms of the idea of Jesus' virgin birth. We could then say that his being the Son of God means that the Holy Spirit fulfilled the role of the male parent in his conception. But he would then be a divine-human figure such as is familiar from Greek mythology; as, for example, Hercules, whose father was the god Jupiter and whose mother was a human woman. However, this has never seriously been regarded as the real meaning of the doctrine of the incarnation. What then is its real meaning? Whenever in the history of Christian thought theologians have tried to spell out its meaning in literal, factual terms the result has been heretical. A classic example would be Apollinaris' theory that Jesus' body and soul were human but that his spirit was the eternal divine Logos. This was rejected as heresy because it implied that Jesus was not genuinely human. And all attempts to treat the incarnation as a factual hypothesis have likewise been rejected by the church because they have failed to do justice either to Jesus' full humanity or to his full deity. Indeed one may say that the fundamental heresy is precisely to treat the incarnation as a factual hypothesis! For the reason why it has never been possible to state a literal meaning for the idea of incarnation is simply that it has no literal meaning. It is a mythological idea, a figure of speech, a piece of poetic imagery. It is a way of saying that Jesus is our living contact with the transcendent God. In his presence we find that we are brought into the presence of God. We believe that he is so truly God's servant that in living as his disciples we are living according to the divine purpose. And as our sufficient and saving point of contact with God there is for us something absolute about him which justifies the absolute language which Christianity has developed. Thus reality is being expressed mythologically when we say that Jesus is the Son of God, God incarnate, the Logos made flesh.

When we see the incarnation as a mythological idea applied to Jesus to express the experienced fact that he is our sufficient, effective, and saving point of contact with God, we no longer have to draw the negative conclusion that he is man's one and only effective point of contact with God. We can revere Christ as the one through whom we have found salvation, without having to deny other points of reported saving contact between God and man. We can commend the way of Christian faith without having to discommend other ways of faith. We can say that there is salvation in Christ without having to say that there is no salvation other than in Christ.

V

Let us return, finally to the historical situation. We have seen that the great world religions arose within different streams of human life and have in the past flowed down the centuries within different cultural channels. They have until recently interacted with one another only spasmodically, and nearly always in hostile clashes rather than in mutual dialogue and friendly interpenetration. But latterly this situation has been changing radically. Since the late nineteenth century there has been a positive influence of Christianity upon Hinduism, bearing fruit in a new social concern in India; and an influence of both Hinduism and Buddhism upon Christianity, bearing fruit in our new Western appreciation of meditation and the arts of spiritual self-development. And today the world religions are increasingly in contact with one another in conscious dialogue and in deliberate attempts to learn about and to learn from one another. These mutual influences can only increase in the future. It is, I think, very important to notice that each of the world religions is in practice an ongoing history of change. Each likes to think of itself as immutable, the same yesterday, today, and forever. But the historian can see that this is not so. Each of the major world faiths has gone through immense historical developments, revolutions, and transformations. Each has experienced times of rapid change, in sudden expansions, schisms, reformations, and renaissances, and also periods of relative stability. Islam has perhaps changed less than the others; but even within Islam there have been immense evolutionary developments and also the growth of important divisions. Hinduism has always been able to change and to absorb new influences into its own life. Christianity and Buddhism have both developed through the centuries almost out of recognition. And in each case there is in principle no limit to the further developments that may take place in the future. In the next period these will occur in a context of interaction. The future of Christianity will be formed partly by influences stemming from Hinduism, Buddhism, and Islam; and this will be so also, in a mutually interactive system, with the other world faiths. And all will be formed partly also by influences stemming from the secular civilization within which they will all exist.

Can we peer into the future and anticipate the pattern of development? Obviously, in trying to do so we are guessing. However, such guessing is today dignified by the name of futurology and large books are written about the state of the planet in, say, the year 2000. These speculations are not random guesses, but are based on the projection of present trends, together with the foreseeable emergence of new trends. If secular seers can speculate in these ways about the future of man, why should we not try to consider the forms which the religious life of mankind will take in, say, a hundred years' time if the present basic trends continue? I am making the very major assumption, which there is no space to defend here, that man's religiousness is innate and that religion will continue in some form so long as human nature remains essentially the same. But what forms will it take? The broad trend of the present century is ecumenical. Old divisions are being transcended. The deeper essentials in which people agree are tending to seem more important than the matters on which they differ. Projecting this trend into the future, we may suppose that the ecumenical spirit which has already so largely transformed Christianity will increasingly affect the relations between the world faiths. There may well be a growing world ecumenism, in which the common commitment of faith in a higher spiritual reality which demands brotherhood on earth will seem more and more significant, while the differences between the religious traditions will seem proportionately less significant. The relation between them may thus become somewhat like that between the Christian denominations in this country—that is to say, they are on increasingly friendly terms; they freely visit one another's worship and are beginning to be able to share places of worship; they cooperate in all sorts of service to the community; their clergy are accustomed to meet together for discussion; and there is even a degree of interchange of ministries; and so on.

What we are picturing here as a future possibility is not a single world religion, but a situation in which the different traditions no longer see themselves and each other as rival ideological communities. A single world religion is, I would think, never likely, and not a consummation to be desired. For so long as there is a variety of human types there will be a variety of kinds of worship and a variety of theological emphases and approaches. There will always be the more mystical and the more prophetic types of faith, with their corresponding awareness of the ultimate Reality as nonpersonal and as personal. There will always be the more spontaneous, warm, and Spirit-filled forms of devotion, and the more liturgical, orderly, and rationally controlled forms. There will always be the more vivid consciousness of the divine on the one hand as gracious love and on the other hand as infinite demand and judgment. And so on. But it is not necessary, and it may in a more ecumenical age not be felt to be necessary, to assume that if God is being truly worshiped by Christians, he cannot also be being truly worshiped by Jews and Muslims and Sikhs and by theistic Hindus and Amida Buddhists; or even that if the ultimate divine Reality is being validly experienced within the theistic streams of religious life as a personal presence, that Reality may not also be validly experienced within other streams of religious life as the infinite Being-Consciousness-Bliss (Satcitananda) of some forms of Hinduism or as the ineffable cosmic Buddha-nature (the Dharmakaya) of some forms of Buddhism. Let me then end with a quotation from one of the great revelatory scriptures of the world: "Howsoever men may approach me, even so do I accept them; for, on all sides, whatever path they may choose is mine." (*Bhagavad-Gita*, IV, 11. On the interpretation of this verse see R. C. Zaehner, *The Bhagavad-Gita*, pp. 185f.; Oxford: The Clarendon Press, 1969.)

V
Sketch for a Global Theory of Religious Knowledge

I hope that this outline sketch—which is currently being developed on a larger scale—of an epistemology intended to apply to the global range of religious traditions will constitute an appropriate salute to Professor Hampus Lyttkens, with his wide philosophical interests, on his sixty-fifth birthday.

The starting point is the religious experience of mankind. This is ostensibly transitive, experience-of. It includes experience of awe in the (supposed) presence of the holy; feelings of creatureliness and dependence in relation to a (supposed) creator; attitudes of abasement and worship, of terror, exaltation, or joy in the presence of the (supposed) divine other; a sense of being addressed, claimed, guided, commanded from beyond oneself; visions of (supposed) divine beings and illuminations concerning (supposedly) transcendent processes and realities; serenity and peace in response to a (supposed) universal presence mediated through nature; the unitive experience of loss of the separate self in a (supposed) infinite whole—as well as yet other, harder to characterize, forms, such as the Zen experience.

It is theoretically possible that this entire range of experience is human projection or fantasy; and it is also theoretically possible that all or some of it is an awareness of a transcendent reality or realities. The basic issue in the philosophy of religion is thus whether religious experience is simply a modification of man's consciousness, generated from within the human mind, or arises from contact with supramundane reality and constitutes cognition, however incomplete and/or distorted, of our more ultimate environment.

It is natural, and indeed biologically necessary, for human beings to assume, in general, that their ostensibly cognitive experience constitutes experience of their environment; for we can only live on the basis of this assumption. Religious belief and practice embody this assumption in relation to religious experience. This application can, however, be questioned on the ground that religious experience produces beliefs that lack the kind of public confirmation available in the case of ordinary perceptual beliefs and scientific hypotheses.

In response to this challenge the basic case for the rationality of religious belief and practice consists in showing (a) the structural continuity of religious awareness with our awareness in other spheres, and (b) that religious beliefs are susceptible to an appropriate kind of experiential confirmation.

a. The key concept which links religious and mundane experience is that of meaning. Meaning is the most general and pervasive characteristic of conscious experience, and it is always relative to a perceiver. The meaning for me of an object or situation consists in the difference that the object or situation, as perceived by me, makes to my dispositional stance in relation to my environment. For A to be aware of an object as being an x, or of a situation in which A is a constituent as being of kind y, is for A to be in a dispositional state to behave in relation to the object on the basis that it is an x, or within the situation on the basis that it is a situation of kind y. This general concept of meaning applies to human cognitive consciousness in general, except perhaps in extreme infancy and in some forms of mental illness. Whether the meaning-seeking functioning of the mind is transcended in mystical consciousness is a major question with important implications for the epistemology of religion.

Awareness of meaning is a product of the interpretative activity of the mind as it becomes conscious of the environment through concepts incarnated in language. Extending Wittgenstein's notion of seeing-as, we can say that all conscious experience (with the possible exceptions noted above) is experiencing-as. At the basic level of ordinary sense perception, I experience this thing as a pen; and one aspect of my so experiencing it is my being in a dispositional state to behave in relation to it in one set of ways rather than another (e.g., to use it to write with rather than to eat with). But our awareness of objects is normally part of a more complex awareness of situations, for objects have their meaning within situational contexts. A situation is a complex of objects attention to which as a whole has its own dispositional significance which is other than the sum of the dispositional significances of its constituent objects. It is at the situational level that we are aware of and interact with other persons, morality being the dispositional aspect of our awareness of the personal world. We are aware of our relationship to others, within the contexts of social life, in ways which we express in the language of ethics. I experience a situation, e.g., as one in which I am conscious of a moral claim upon me to help this person who is in danger. Thus the level of interpretation at which we are aware of the ethical meaning of situations presupposes, and is of a logically higher order than, the level of ordinary sensory interpretation, at which we are aware of the natural world which constitutes (though it does not only constitute) the setting of the moral life. The further level of interpretation at which we are aware of the religious meaning of some of life's situations, or of our total life situation, likewise presupposes both the natural level and the ethical level of meaning. (There are, however, important differences to be noted between the forms of religious meaning awareness of which is cultivated within different religious traditions.)

Meaning, defined in dispositional terms, always involves action—including the apparent inaction that consists in going on doing the same thing. For our dispositional stance reflects our purposes as well as our perception of the world. It thus has a teleological aspect and presupposes time as the dimension of change. Religious experience, as the awareness of the religious meaning of situations, is likewise related to time and is eschatological in character—either in terms of the outer eschatology of a divine purpose moving through history to its fulfillment in the "kingdom of God," or the inner eschatology of the development of the individual spirit to its final self-transcendence in Nirvana or in Buddhahood or in unity with Brahman. In each case our present life has overall meaning as a movement through time toward the eschaton, variously thought of as enhancement of meaning in the life of the heavenly kingdom, or as transcendence of meaning, either beyond activity, purposes, and change, or within the evanescent process itself.

b. It is in virtue of its eschatological character that religious belief can be seen to be making verifiable claims concerning the actual character of the universe. For the religions affirm either that the universe is in process toward a future state of perfection or that the individual is in process toward a future state of self-transcending enlightenment or liberation; and the progressive fulfillment of this expectation can confirm the system of belief of which it is a part to a point that puts it beyond rational doubt. It may of course be that currently held systems of belief will be partly confirmed and partly refuted in future experience, so that there will be a development of belief rather than a simple verification of present convictions.

At this point we have to take note of the problem posed by the plurality of religious traditions. Having argued for the rationality of religious belief and practice on the basis of the acceptance of religious experience as genuine contact with transcendent reality, we are faced with the very diverse, and apparently conflicting, beliefs and practices of the various traditions. The basic hypothesis which suggests itself is that the different streams of religious experience represent diverse awarenesses of the same transcendent reality, which is perceived in characteristically different ways by different human mentalities, formed by and forming different cultural histories.

Proceeding inductively from the plurality of forms of religious experience, accepted as variously cognitive (and miscognitive) of transcendent reality, we have to distinguish between that transcendent reality *an sich* and as it is experienced by human beings. Let us call the former the Eternal One—a term which draws ambivalently upon two different sets of associations: on the one hand the mystical One of Plotinus and the One without a second of the Upanishads, and on the other hand the One who is the divine Thou of the biblical narratives. For the Eternal One, as the ultimate transcendent reality, both lies beyond human experience and conceptuality and, at the same time, is the ground of all dependent being, including personal beings. The Eternal One is thus the divine noumenon which is experienced and thought within the different religious traditions as the range of divine phenomena witnessed to by the religious history of mankind.

The philosophical framework here is Kantian, but with the proviso that the phenomenal world *is* the noumenal world as humanly experienced. The result is the distinctly non-Kantian thesis that the divine is experienced (rather than postulated, as Kant believed), but is experienced within the limitations of our human cognitive apparatus in ways analogous to that in which he argued that we experience our physical environment.

The hypothesis has to be spelled out in relation both (1) to theistic and (2) to nontheistic religious awareness.

1. Man's religious experience, which is for the most part theistic, speaks of an immense plurality of (polytheistic) gods and (monotheistic) Gods. We can concentrate

upon the issues raised by the plurality of monotheistic faiths, each witnessing to a supreme personal being.

On the modern understanding of personality as essentially interpersonal, God can be said to be personal only in relation to created persons. (The Christian concept of God as Trinity has to be considered here, as a possible way of avoiding this conclusion.) A personal God is thus an essentially historical being who exists as such in interpersonal relationship with the community that worships him. Thus, e.g., Yahweh is a different person, with a different concrete character, from Krishna, the two having different personal histories formed in interaction with different communities, with their different cultural forms of life. Our hypothesis is that each is the Eternal One experienced as concretely personal by and in relation to a different human community.

But while the various divine *personae* have their personal existence only in relation to their worshipers, they have in that relationship a public and historical reality. In each case the divine *persona* that is being worshiped represents the Eternal One as experienced through the filter of a human religious tradition, within which men, in their variously imperfect spiritual and moral states, can be both sustained and challenged by the divine reality.

2. Rather than speak of the nontheistic religions, one should speak of the nontheistic forms of religion which occur, most prominently, within Hinduism, Buddhism, Taoism, and Confucianism. In these nontheistic forms of religious experience and thought—according to our hypothesis—the Eternal One is known and responded to in nonpersonal terms, as the depth or ground of being, as the Infinite, or the Absolute (Brahman), as Nirvana, as Sunyata ("Voidness"), and in yet other ways. Thus, for advaitic Hinduism, the noumenal human self (atman) knows the divine noumenon (Atman), which it ultimately is, not in a subject-object relationship but in the unitive

self-awareness which is final liberation. Theravada Buddhism centers upon the experience of Nirvana, the indescribable reality that is attained through realization of the insubstantiality of the self and through cessation of the desires that bind us to the suffering process of *samsara*. In Mahayana Buddhism there is generally a different emphasis: the aim is Buddhahood or, more precisely, to become a bodhisattva, for whom *samsara* and Nirvana are one, and who can thus accept the world and inhabit it in a new way, without illusion, finding in its very lack of unephemeral being the ultimate reality of Sunyata. In each case there is a change in the human being in virtue of which he is, or knows, or participates in reality at first hand.

Two very different interpretations are possible of this latter state. According to one (i), this ultimate experience is a direct awareness of reality *an sich*, not mediated—or, therefore, distorted—by the perceptual machinery of the human mind; and in contrast, from this point of view, theistic religion exhibits a lower and preliminary form of spiritual awareness, in which the human ego projects and worships the divine Ego.

According to the alternative interpretation (ii), even the apparently direct and undistorted awareness of reality in the advaitic *moksha*, in the Buddhist *satori*, and in unitive mysticism, is still the conscious experience of a human subject, and is as such influenced by the interpretative set of the cognizing mind. For every human being has been influenced by the culture of which he is a part, and has received, or has developed in his individual appropriation of it, certain deep interpretative tendencies which help to form, and are thus continually confirmed within, his experience. We see evidence of such deep "sets" at work when we observe that mystics formed by Hindu, Buddhist, Christian, Muslim, and other religious cultures report distinctively different forms of experience. So far from its being the case that they all undergo an identical experience, but report it in different religious languages, it seems more probable that they undergo characteristically different unitive experiences (even though with important common features), the differences being caused by the conceptual frameworks and meditational disciplines supplied by the religious traditions in which they participate.

The unitive mystic within a particular tradition cannot, of course, simply qua adherent of that tradition, grant that the form taken by his own experience has been determined by anything other than the reality which he is cognizing. But in the light of the comparative study of religions it seems likely that his own experience, as well as that of others, is in fact mediated through a particular interpretative framework. It may be that there is an eschatological state, beyond individual embodiment, in which consciousness is no longer interpretative in character; but it would seem that the consciousness of the embodied mind, operating through the mechanism of the physical brain, must always—even in the case of the most advanced mystics—be the outcome of an active interpretative process.

Accordingly, the nontheistic and theistic forms of experience may well exhibit a common epistemological structure. They will then appear as alternative, and perhaps equally valid, perceptions of the Eternal One, rather than as, respectively, totally veridical and relatively illusory perceptions of it.

Finally, it is our human capacity to misperceive the Eternal One, partially excluding it from consciousness, that makes possible our freedom as finite creatures in relation to it. There is a continual presence of the Eternal One to mankind, mediated particularly through receptive spirits, the saints, mahatmas, arahants, gurus, prophets, and messiahs through whose work the various traditions have developed over the centuries. The broad differences between these traditions, and between their different images of the Eternal One, arise from the broad differences between human cultures—differences whose roots are many and complex and have been as yet only very partially traced by the historians and anthropologists.

VI
Toward a Philosophy
of Religious Pluralism

From the point of view of phenomenology, or description, the fact of religious pluralism presents no philosophical problem. It just is the case that there are many different traditions of religious life and thought. Their histories, and their interactions with one another and with other aspects of the human story, have been traced in increasing detail during the last hundred and fifty years or so; and indeed knowledge of the religious life of mankind has now multiplied to the point at which it far exceeds the receptivity of any one mind. There is available to us a fascinating plethora of information concerning religious practices and beliefs, worship and ethics, creeds and theologies, myths, poetry, music, and architecture, reported religious and mystical experiences, and the interactions of all these with one another. But simply as historical fact none of this raises a *problem* of religious pluralism. It is only when we add what can be called the basic religious conviction that a problem is generated.

By the basic religious conviction I mean the conviction that the realm of religious experience and belief is our human response to a transcendent divine reality or realities. It is the conviction, in other words, that religion is not, as a totality, illusion and self-deception. Whether this conviction is justified and, if so, how that justification is to be spelled out is the central issue in the philosophy of religion; and on other occasions I have, together with many others, addressed myself to that issue. But in this chapter I propose to consider a further problem which arises if one adopts that basic religious conviction. One may actually share that conviction (as I do), or one may simply be interested to see what the implications of religious pluralism are for religious belief. But on whichever basis, let us, for the purposes of the present discussion, assume hypothetically the truth of the basic religious conviction and ask ourselves how the facts of religious pluralism may then be understood.

The basic religious conviction normally takes the form of the claim that some one particular religion is a valid response to the divine, a response embodying true beliefs concerning the nature of reality. And the problem of religious pluralism arises from the fact that there are many such claims. In view of this variety of gospels it would seem on the face of it that they cannot all be true; and in that case may they not very well all be false? This is the problem that is generated by the fact of religious pluralism in conjunction with the basic religious conviction.

However, in adopting the basic religious conviction we are not obliged to assume that all religious experience is straightforwardly veridical or that all religious belief is straightforwardly true. On the contrary, our human nature and circumstances may well make their own contribution to our religious awareness, a contribution in which the range of individual and social mentalities and of cultural forms produces a corresponding variety of perceptions—or, it may be, of partial distortions—in our human consciousness of the divine. But we are nevertheless assuming that, basically, religion is a range of responses to reality—even if variously inadequate responses—rather than being pure projection or illusion.

Clearly this assumption must, unless good reasons to the contrary are produced, be applied to the entire realm of religions and not only to one favored religion. I cannot then, as a Christian, solve the problem of religious pluralism by holding that my own religion is a response to the divine reality but that the others are merely human projections. I cannot say, with Karl Barth, that "the Christian religion is true, because it has pleased God, who alone can be the judge in this matter, to affirm it to be the true religion," so that "it alone has the commission and the authority to be a missionary religion, i.e., to confront the world of religions as the one true religion, with absolute self-confidence to invite and challenge it to abandon its ways and to start on the Christian way" (*Church Dogmatics*, I/2, pp. 350, 357). Such sublime bigotry could only be possible for one who had no real interest in or awareness of the wider religious life of mankind. For it is evident, when one witnesses worship within the great world faiths, including Christianity, that the same sort of thing is going on in each, namely the directing of the worshipers' attention upon a (putative) higher and transcendent reality, in relation to which lies the human being's ultimate good. There may be clear and convincing criteria by which some forms of religion can be seen to be "better" or "higher" than others. But if we restrict our attention to the great world traditions, the only criterion by which any of these could be judged to be the one and only true religion, with all the others dismissed as false, would be its own dogmatic assertion, in its more chauvinistic moments, to this effect.

Let us then look at the religious scene and consider how its pluralism is to be understood.

At the outset we encounter a terminological problem to which there seems to be no satisfactory solution. How are we to name the postulated transcendent reality to which we are assuming that religion is man's response? One is initially inclined to reject the word "God" as too theistic—for the religious spectrum includes major non-theistic as well as theistic traditions—and to consider such alternatives as "the Transcendent," "the Divine," "the Dharma," "the Absolute," "the Tao," "Being-it-self," "Brahman," "the ultimate divine Reality." The fact is, however, that we have no fully tradition-neutral or tradition-transcending term. One is therefore obliged to use a term provided by a particular tradition, but to use it (or consciously to misuse it) in a way which moves beyond the bounds of that tradition. As a Christian I shall accordingly use the word "God," but shall not use it in a straightforwardly theistic sense. There is of course a danger that either the writer or the reader may slip back, without noticing it, into the standard use of the term; and both must try to be vigilant against this. I shall then, in what follows, speak of God, but with the important proviso that it is an open question at this stage whether, and if so in what sense, God is personal. We shall in fact, I believe, be led to distinguish between God, and God as conceived and experienced by human beings. God is neither a person nor a thing, but is the transcendent reality which is conceived and experienced by different human mentalities in both personal and nonpersonal ways.

The general conception of a distinction between, on the one hand, the Godhead in its own infinite depths beyond human experience and comprehension and, on the other hand, the Godhead as finitely experienced by humanity is both ancient and widespread. Perhaps its most explicit form is the Hindu distinction between *nirguna* Brahman, Brahman without attributes, beyond the scope of human language, and *saguna* Brahman, Brahman with attributes, known within human religious experience as Ishvara, the personal creator and governor of the universe. In the West the Christian mystic Meister Eckhart distinguished between the Godhead *(Deitas)* and God *(Deus)*; and Rudolf Otto, in his comparative study of Eckhart and Shankara, says, "Herein lies the most extraordinary analogy between Eckhart and Sankara: high above God and the personal Lord abides the 'Godhead,' having an almost identical relationship to God as that of Brahman to Isvara" (*Mysticism East and West;* Meridian Books, p. 14). The Taoist scripture, the

Tao Te Ching, begins by affirming that "the Tao that can be expressed is not the eternal Tao." The Jewish Cabalist mystics distinguished between En Soph, the absolute divine reality beyond human description, and the God of the Bible; and among the Sufis, Al Haqq, the Real, seems to be a similar concept, as the abyss of Godhead underlying the personal Allah. More recently Paul Tillich has spoken of "the God above the God of theism" (*The Courage to Be,* p. 190; Yale University Press, 1952) and has said that "God is the symbol of God" (*The Dynamics of Faith,* p. 46; Harper & Brothers, 1957). Whitehead and the process theologians who have followed him distinguish between the primordial and the consequent nature of God, the former being his nature in himself, and the latter being constituted by his inclusion of and response to the world. And Gordon Kaufman has recently distinguished between the "real God" and the "available God," the former being an "utterly unknowable X" and the latter being "essentially a mental or imaginative construction" (*God the Problem,* p. 86; Harvard University Press, 1972). A traditional Christian form of the distinction is that between God in himself, in his infinite self-existent being, beyond the grasp of the human mind, and God in relation to mankind, revealed as creator and redeemer. In one form or another such a distinction seems unavoidable for any view which is not willing to reduce God to a finite being, wholly knowable by the human mind and definable in human concepts. The infinite God must pass out into sheer mystery beyond the reach of our knowledge and comprehension, and is in this limitless transcendence *nirguna,* the ultimate Godhead, the God above the God of theism.

There are in fact, I would suggest, three main types of religious experience. The most common is the experience of God as a personal presence and will, known in I-Thou encounter. This experience is the heart of theistic religion, in the Eastern as well as in the Western traditions. The second type is the nature—or cosmic—mysticism in which the whole world or the whole universe is experienced as the manifestation or vehicle of divine reality—as in Wordsworth's famous lines:

> And I have felt
> A presence that disturbs me with the
>   joy
> Of elevated thoughts; a sense sublime
> Of something far more deeply inter-
>   fused,
> Whose dwelling is the light of setting
>   suns,
> And the round ocean and the living air,
> And the blue sky, and in the mind of
>   man:
> A motion and a spirit, that impels
> All thinking things, all objects of all
>   thought,
> And rolls through all things.

In such experiences God is not known as personal, nor yet as impersonal, but rather as more than personal—as living, as the ultimate source of value, and yet as altogether transcending the notion of an encountered person, on however tremendous a scale. And the third type is that in which the experiencing self is temporarily absorbed into the divine reality, becoming one with the One. Since personality is essentially interpersonal, so that one is a person only in relationship with other persons, there is no personal existence or encounter within this unitive moment. This is perhaps the mystical state *par excellence*, apparently experienced by some, but described by none; for it is beyond the scope of human language.

Now these are all finite experiences of finite creatures. (This is true even of the unitive experience; for the experiencer returns from it, still a finite individual, to try to speak of what has happened to him.) If we assume, with the major religious traditions, that God is infinite, then we have to say that these forms of religious experience are not experiences of the infinitude of God—which no finite experience could ever encompass—but of God as finitely experienced by particular human consciousnesses. And in understanding such a plurality of experiences we have to take account of the contribution of the human mind itself to all our awareness of our environment, divine as well as natural. I shall be arguing that these different forms of religious awareness are not necessarily competitive, in the sense that the validity of one entails the spuriousness of the others, but that they are better understood as different phenomenal experiences of the one divine noumenon, or, in another language, as different experiential transformations of the same transcendent informational input.

I shall return in due course to the nonpersonal forms of religious awareness; but let us first approach the idea of a divine phenomenon through the theistic type of religious experience.

If one were to list all the many gods whose names we know from the literature and traditions of India (such as Rudra, Agni, Mitra, Indra, Varuna) and of the Near East (such as Osiris, Isis, Horus, Ra, Yahweh) and of southern Europe (such as Jupiter, Apollo, Dionysus, Poseidon) and of northern Europe (such as Odin, Thor, Balder, Vali, Woden) and of Africa (such as Nabongo, Luhanga, Nyame, Lesa, Ruhanga) and also of the Americas, Australasia, northern Asia, and the rest of the world, they would probably form a list as long as the telephone directory of a large city. What are we to say about all these gods? Do we say that they all exist? And what would it be for a named god, say Balder, with his distinctive characteristics, to exist? In any straightforward sense it would, I suggest, at least involve there being a consciousness, answering to this name, in addition to all the millions of human consciousnesses. Are we then to say that for each name in our directory of gods there is an additional consciousness enjoying the further set of attributes specified by the concept of that particular god? In most cases this would be theoretically possible, since in most cases the gods are explicitly or implicitly finite beings whose powers and spheres of operation are at least approximately known; and many of them could coexist without contradiction. On the other hand, the gods of the monotheistic faiths are thought of in each case as the one and only God, so that it is impossible for more than one of them to instantiate this concept. It does not seem, then, that we can possibly say that all the named gods, and particularly not all the most important ones, exist, at any rate not in any simple and straightforward sense. Nor, having assumed the basic religious conviction of the reality of the divine, can we say in any straightforward sense that they are all nonexistent and man's whole supposed awareness of divine beings and powers is illusory. Nor again, as I have already indicated, can we take refuge in the claim that the God of one's own religion is real and all the others are either illusory or, perhaps, nondivine, demonic beings. Instead let us explore the possibility that the immediate object of theistic religious awareness is what I shall call an "image" of God, and that the plurality of such images arises from the various ways in which the divine reality has impinged upon the human consciousness in its different circumstances.

But first we must establish the distinction between God and our human images of God. Within the Judeo-Christian tradition we see the need for such a distinction when we ask ourselves whether God is really male, as distinguished from female, or whether on the contrary God transcends the distinction between men and women but has commonly been thought of as male within patriarchal societies. I believe that most of us today will give the latter answer. Although in the Bible God is consistently referred to as "he" and is described, metaphorically, as king, father, warrior, shepherd, etc., yet surely God is not in fact a larger or even an infinite man as distinguished from woman, but can be thought of equally appropriately in male and female terms. In this respect much Indian devotional language, in which God is addressed as mother as well as father, is to be preferred to the exclusively masculine language of the Semitic faiths. But the point at the moment is that if God is not in reality male as distinguished from female, but is nevertheless imaged as such in many religious traditions, then we are obliged to draw a distinction between God and our human images of God—in this case between God and our distinctively masculine images of God.

But what, more precisely, do we mean by an "image" of God? We can, I think, find partial analogies in the varied impressions of the same individual in the minds of different historians. Consider a personage, X, who lived in the past and who is therefore not directly accessible to us, about whom certain salient facts are known but such that any concrete impression of X's character leaves a good deal to the constructive imagination of the historian. Any such impression or, as I shall call it, image represents an interpretation of the available data. Varying images of X may form in the minds of writers in different subsequent periods, with their different cultural backgrounds; and there may be both popular, often oversimplified, images and caricatures as well as more academic images. There are a number of famous historical figures to whom all this applies—for example, Mary Queen of Scots, King Charles I, Napoleon, Abraham Lincoln, Mahatma Gandhi, Stalin, Chairman Mao. In such cases the distinction seems inevitable between the historical individual *an sich* and the images in terms of which he or she has become known to later consciousness. This is of course only a partial analogy; I am not suggesting that God existed in the past but does not exist today. The analogy is rather with the varying images in terms of which we may be aware of a historical figure. An image of this kind represents data molded into concrete forms by the imagination in accordance with the selective attention of the historian. And the more a figure

engages our interest by touching our own vital concerns—for example, a concern for justice or freedom—
the greater tends to be the subjective contribution to our
image of him or her. And when we turn to those who are
religiously significant to us, and who accordingly help to
form the basic orientation of our lives, the subjective
contribution generally increases yet further in importance. Because a saint, or messiah, or avatar, or bodhisattva, or arahant, or spiritual master, or guru meets some
spiritual need in us, and so has salvific power in our
lives, our image of such a person naturally emphasizes
holiness, goodness, wisdom, and remarkable powers;
and further the image tends to expand as the tradition in
which it is embedded develops. These images of saints—
and I am referring to personality impressions of them
rather than to physical representations—extend the analogy in the direction of our images of God. Within
Christianity, Catholic spirituality is particularly rich in
examples. The faithful often address an individual saint,
or Mary, mother of Jesus, asking him or her to perform
some miracle or to intercede for them with God the
Father. In the case of Mary, distinctive local versions are
cherished within particular communities. Thus there is
Our Lady of Lourdes, who appeared as a young girl
eighteen times to Bernadette Soubirous in 1858, speaking to her on several occasions, thereby founding a place
of pilgrimage and healing to which many thousands go
each year. There is Our Lady of Fatima, in Portugal, who
made prophecies about when the First World War was to
end, about developments in Russia, and about another
war in the future. And there is Our Lady of Walsingham,
as well as other local miraculous versions of Mary in
many countries. Thus if we assume that the Virgin Mary
is an existing personal being, now exalted into heaven
but still actively concerned with the affairs of living men
and women, we are led to distinguish between Mary
herself and a variety of partially different human images
of her. It does not, however, necessarily follow from the

fact of their plurality that these images are false. The alternative possibility is that they arise from genuine encounters with Mary in which, as she has met the varying needs of different individuals and communities, different images of her have legitimately been formed.

An analogy even closer to our images of God is provided, within Christianity, by the different images of Christ. For the historical Jesus is a prime example of someone who has given rise to a range of images expressing a variety of interpretative responses. He has, for example, been perceived, or imaged, or responded to as God incarnate; as a human teacher of the fatherhood of God and the brotherhood of man; as an apocalyptic preacher of the imminent end of history; as "gentle Jesus meek and mild"; as a social radical proclaiming that the lowly are to be exalted and the mighty brought down; as the "man for others," the embodiment of self-giving love; and of course as various mixtures of these. Different popular images of Jesus are expressed in the growing number of interpretations of him in films and rock operas. Merely to list these different Jesuses of the religious and secular imagination is to recognize a distinction between the historical individual who lived in Galilee nineteen centuries ago, concerning whom we have rather few items of secure information, and the plurality of images of him operating in the minds of different individuals and groups and communal traditions. But beyond this, the historical Jesus has expanded in Christian thought and experience into two further Christ figures who are distinct (in that they have been able to operate within different streams of spirituality) and yet also capable of merging into one (in yet other forms of spirituality). One of these is the cosmic Christ, the eternal divine Son, "seated at the right hand of the Father" as the second Person of the holy Trinity. This cosmic Christ has been imaged in very different ways in different periods of history and in different branches of the church—as the imperial Pantocrator, as Victor over the devil, as the terrible Judge before whom his mother had to intercede for human sinners, and often in the modern church as the spirit of divine love. But given this plurality of images there remains the possibility that they represent different and partial human awareness of the same transcendent cosmic being. The other Christ figure is the personal Jesus-presence reported by many Christians as a living being to whom they speak and who in some manner speaks to them and sometimes directs their lives. This presence may be known at any one time to a number of different Christians in different places, being experienced in varying ways related to their personal situations and needs. The object of each believer's consciousness, in these cases, is his or her own image of Jesus; and the question which again remains open is whether these images are simply projections of the imagination or are joint creations of human imagination and an informing input from the living person of Jesus. It seems clear that to some extent Christians each have their own images of the risen Lord; but it remains possible that the risen Jesus is meeting them and interacting with them, in ways related to their own spiritual needs and capacities, through these different images of him. But whatever ontological status we attribute to the different versions of the Jesus-presence and of the cosmic Christ, we are obliged to recognize a distinction between this plurality of images and the person whose images they are.

A further analogy, which may be illuminating to some, even though possibly not to others, comes from parapsychology. One of the types of phenomena studied is that in which a medium goes into a trance and it seems that the still-living consciousness of someone who has physically died—let us call him John Smith—communicates through the medium's vocal machinery. Sometimes the "spirit" speaks in a way which is recognizably that of the John Smith who he claims to be, and sometimes also his conversation includes items of information which could hardly have been known to the medium. To account for all this the theory has been advanced that the conscious, speaking, responding personality who is controlling the medium's vocal apparatus is a secondary personality, a fragment of the medium's mind which takes over in the trance state. This secondary personality plays roles suggested to it and indeed often puts considerable intelligence and skill into its productions—somewhat as in the case of hypnotized persons, who may play on command the role of, say, guests at a banquet or visitors from outer space. In the spiritualist séance it may be that the informational input which informs the performance is derived telepathically from the sitters. But the further possibility has been suggested that some of the input may come from the deceased individual John Smith, who is being impersonated by the medium's secondary personality. In that case John Smith is, in this doubtless frustratingly indirect and unreliable way, communicating with his friends on earth. If this is so, the sitters are in contact with a dramatic personation of John Smith, produced by a secondary personality of the medium, but based at least partly on information deriving from John Smith himself. Thus it is possible that he communicates at different times to different groups of sitters through varying dramatic images of himself formed in the minds of different mediums. Here again we are led to a distinction between John Smith *an sich* and a plurality of, in this case, speaking and responding images of him which are partly similar and partly different.

I do not want to pursue here the possible functional analogy between spiritualist mediums and the prophets, avatars, gurus, etc., through whom God is believed to speak to mankind. I want instead to develop a different aspect of the theory of mediumship to which I have referred. In doing so it will be helpful to use the notion of information, not in the familiar propositional sense of "items of information" but in the modern cybernetic sense of cognitive input which can be expressed in different modes and which can be transformed from one mode to another. The value of this concept lies precisely in its generality. Whatever influences or impacts from our surrounding world affect one's state as a self-directing part of that world constitute information. In the definition of Norbert Wiener, the father of cybernetics: "Information is a name for the content of what is exchanged with the outer world as we adjust to it, and make our adjustment felt upon it." (*The Human Use of Human Beings*, p. 19; London: Sphere Books, 1968.) Thus information passes in the form of light waves from a lighted object to the retina of the eye, is there transformed into chemical changes in the rods and cones, and then into electrical impulses passing up the strands of the optic nerve into the brain, and finally into the conscious experience of seeing the object which had been reflecting light into our eye. Or again, information flows along the wire from the aerial into the television set and is there transformed into a picture on the screen; or along the telephone wire to be transformed into the sound of a voice. In such cases the same information is being expressed in a variety of ways. And whenever there is transformation from one coding to another there is the possibility of distortion of the information. Indeed there is a general tendency for information to deteriorate as it functions. The picture on the television screen may be distorted or blurred; and the machinery of the brain can likewise be damaged and produce a distorted version of the environment in consciousness. These are mechanical failures, comparable with the errors to which an electronic calculator is liable when its battery is insufficiently charged. But in addition to the mechanical transformation of information studied by cybernetics there is also, and more importantly, its interpretation by the mind into units or moments of meaning. For at the distinctively human level of consciousness we inhabit a more or less familiar and ordered world with recognizable characteristics to which we know how to respond. (There is of course also novelty and surprise, but always within the context of a familiar basic framework.) All our consciousness of objects and of situations is our experience of them as having a certain character, such that it is appropriate to behave in relation to them, or within them, in this rather than that way. Such awareness represents a fusion between, on the one hand, the information reaching us from our environment and, on the other hand, the system of concepts in terms of which that information comes to consciousness as organized and meaningful experience. In this procedure—which constitutes normal perception—the function of our system of concepts, or recognitional capacities, is to guide the preconscious interpretative process whereby sensory information is transformed into our actual consciousness of the world. The word "meaning" is appropriate as pointing to the way in which our awareness of our environment, as having the character that we experience it to have, is related to our own practical responses to it. To say that the perceived world has meaning to us is to say that it is a world which we can inhabit by acting and reacting in accordance with its perceived character. For meaning, in this sense, is meaning for someone; it is the difference which awareness of the presence of this particular thing, or of being in this particular environing situation, makes to the perceiver's dispositional stance. Thus, to be conscious that the object which I am now holding in my hand is a pen is to be in a distinctive dispositional state in relation to it, such that I expect it to make marks in ink but not to bite or talk, and such that I shall use it for writing but not normally for any other purpose. And in general our awareness of our environment as having the complex character that we perceive it to have consists in part in our being in a correspondingly complex dispositional state in relation to it.

This general account of cognition also applies to our awareness (whether veridical or illusory) of the religious meaning, or character, of situations. For our human commerce with God does not consist only or even mainly in our holding certain beliefs, but above all in experiencing the reality of God as the lord in whose presence one is, and in experiencing the power of God in the events of one's own life and of the wider history with which this is continuous. When, for example, Jeremiah perceived the Babylonian army, which was marching on Jersusalem, as God's agent to punish his unfaithful people, he was interpreting the events of his time in terms of his image of God, this interpretation coming to consciousness in his awareness of God as actively at work in the events of the world around him, and having its dispositional correlate in his inner compulsion to proclaim the religious meaning of these events. Or when today a theistic believer has some degree of awareness of existing in the unseen presence of God, he is interpreting his total situation in religious terms. This interpretation comes to consciousness as the experience that in and through all his dealings with the world and with other people he is also having to do with the transcendent God; and this awareness is embodied in his dispositional state in, for example, tendencies to engage in acts of worship, to think and feel in certain ways, and to behave in accordance with associated ethical norms.

What part, then, is played in this religious awareness by images of God? Essentially the part, I suggest, that is played in sense perception by the concepts or recognitional capacities in terms of which we are conscious of the objects and situations constituting our physical environment.

It was above all Immanuel Kant, with his doctrine that we are necessarily aware of the world in terms of certain forms and categories inherent in the structure of a unitary finite consciousness, who enabled the modern world to recognize the mind's own positive contribution to the meaningful character of its perceived environment. The view that I am proposing is in some respects Kantian and in other respects un-Kantian, and it may perhaps be useful at this point to bring out the analogies and disanalogies with the Kantian model. Kant is himself notoriously difficult to interpret, largely because the *Critique of Pure Reason* contains several different strands of argument whose mutual consistency can be questioned and whose relative importance can be variously estimated. The strand that I shall be using is the distinction between phenomenon and noumenon, but transposed from the problem of sense perception to that of the awareness of God. In using something analogous to Kant's phenomenon/noumenon distinction I am not opting for any view of the place of this distinction in the *Critique of Pure Reason*. I am in fact not concerned at all with questions of Kantian interpretation or of the general assessment of Kant's critical philosophy. I am, rather, taking a structural model from his system and using it in a sphere—the epistemology of religion—which Kant treated in a very different way, and I am using it in relation to a problem within that sphere which had hardly begun to be recognized in his time. It should also be stressed that Kant himself would not have sanctioned the idea that we in any way *experience* God, even as divine phenomenon in distinction from divine noumenon. For him God was not a reality encountered in religious experience, but an object postulated by reason on the basis of its own practical functioning as moral agent. The reality of moral obligation presupposes the reality of God as the basis of the possibility of the *summum bonum* in which perfect goodness and perfect happiness coincide. God must accordingly be postulated as "a cause of the whole of nature, itself distinct from nature, which contains the ground of the exact coincidence of happiness with morality" (*Critique of Practical Reason*, Book II, Ch. V, p. 125). The idea of God, thus indirectly established, also functions as a regulative idea whereby we "regard all order in the world *as if* it had originated in the purpose of a supreme reason" (*Critique of Pure Reason*, Appendix to the Transcendental Dialectic, p. B 714). Thus for Kant

God is not experienced, but postulated. However, I am exploring here the different and very non-Kantian hypothesis that God *is* experienced by human beings, but experienced in a manner analogous to that in which, according to Kant, we experience the world—namely by informational input from external reality being interpreted by the mind in terms of its own categorial system and thus coming to consciousness as meaningful phenomenal experience. For Kant distinguished—in one strand of his thought—between the noumenal world, which exists independently of and outside man's perception of it, and the phenomenal world, which is that world as it appears to our human consciousness. All that we are entitled to say about the noumenal world is that it is the unknown reality whose informational input produces, in collaboration with the human mind, the phenomenal world of our experience. This happens through the medium of certain concepts which Kant calls the categories of the Understanding. In Kant's system the pure categories, or pure concepts of the Understanding (for example, substance), are schematized in terms of temporality to produce the more concrete categories which are exhibited in our actual experience of the world. (For example, the pure concept of substances is schematized as the concept of an object enduring through time.) Something analogous to this, I am suggesting, takes place in our awareness of God. For the religious person experiences the divine, not as a general idea, but under some specific and relatively concrete divine image. An abstract concept of deity, such as the concept of "the uncreated creator of the universe," is schematized or concretized in a range of divine images. And if we ask what functions in a role analogous to that of time in the schematization of the Kantian categories, the answer, I suggest, is the continuum of historical factors which have produced our different religious cultures. It is the variations of the human cultural situation that concretize the notion of deity as specific images of God. And it is these images that inform man's actual religious experience, so that it is an experience specifically of the God of Israel, or of Allah, or of the Father of our Lord Jesus Christ, or of Vishnu or Shiva.

It is desirable to avoid a possible misunderstanding which offers itself at this point. If the worshiper's thought of God only describes an image of God, and the worshiper's experience of God is only the experience of God as thus imaged, does it not follow that worship is directed to an illusion, a mere phenomenal appearance? The answer must echo Kant's statement that his distinction between phenomenon, or appearance, and noumenon, or reality, results in a "transcendental idealism" which is at the same time an "empirical realism" (*Critique of Pure Reason*, pp. A 370–372). That is to say, the world as we perceive it is real, not illusory; but it is the appearance to us of that which exists in itself outside our experience of it. The perceptually organized world of colors, sounds, and scents, of heat and cold, of solid tables and chairs and trees and animals, is entirely real. And yet, as humanly perceived, it exists only for human perceivers. Animals with different sensory equipment and different forms of consciousness must perceive the world very differently. We are real beings in a real environment; but we experience that environment selectively, in terms of our special cognitive equipment. Something essentially similar has to be said about the human awareness of God. God as experienced by this or that individual or group is real, not illusory; and yet the experience of God is partial and is adapted to our human spiritual capacities. God as humanly known is not God *an sich* but God in relation to mankind, thought of and experienced in terms of some particular limited tradition of religious awareness and response. Thus in expounding this situation we have to try to keep two themes in balance: the agnostic theme that we only know God partially and imperfectly, and the positive theme that we really do know God as practically and savingly related to ourselves.

Let us now apply this thesis to what is perhaps the

largest and most obvious contrast between different
human awarenesses of the divine, namely as personal
and as nonpersonal.

A number of Christian theologians have distinguished
between "being a person" and "being personal," the
theological point of the distinction lying in their assumption that whereas a person is necessarily finite, a personal being may be infinite. However, the distinction is
entirely stipulative and has no further use than to avoid
the problems connected with the concept of an infinite
person. To be personal, surely, is to be a person: the
notion of a personal being who is not a person has no
content. Accordingly the idea of an infinite personal
being is the same as the idea of an infinite person. It is
not easy to determine whether this idea is viable, and I
do not want to argue the question here. Instead I propose
to take account of the modern insight that personality is
essentially interpersonal. The medieval concept of a
person was that of "an individual rational substance"
(Boethius). On this definition it is conceivable for there
to be only one person in existence; a person does not
inherently need there to be other persons in relation to
whom one is oneself a person. On this view we can
conceive of God, "prior to" and independently of his
creation, as the eternal and infinite person. But this
notion collapses if we adopt the modern understanding
of personality as a function of community. On this view,
to be a person is to exist in personal interaction with
other persons; and the idea of a person existing *a se*, as
the only person in existence, is a self-contradiction.
Clearly, this understanding of personality makes it impossible to think of God as eternally personal in his own
self-existent being, "prior" and without relation to his
creation.

But cannot this particular problem be met by invoking
the Christian conception that God is three Persons in
one? This doctrine has taken a variety of forms within the
long Christian tradition, ranging from the virtual trithe-

ism of the "social" conceptions of the Trinity to the modalistic notion of three modes of operation of the one God. The latter, while in many ways attractive, does not enable us to speak of interpersonal relationships between the hypostases of the Trinity, or thus to speak of the Godhead as inherently and eternally personal. A society of three, sustaining personal relationships between its members, requires three centers of personal consciousness and will, however harmoniously related. Such virtual tritheism is found not only in popular understandings and artistic representations of the Trinity but also within patristic thought, particularly among the Cappadocian fathers of the fourth century. Thus Gregory of Nazianzus used the example of Adam, Eve, and their son Seth, who were three and yet shared the same human nature, as an analogy for the Father, Son, and Spirit, who are three while sharing the same divine nature. This kind of Trinitarianism does enable us to think of the Godhead, in its eternal nature independently of the creation, as containing personality; for on this interpretation the Godhead consists of three interrelated personal beings forming together a uniquely intimate divine society. But it cannot be concealed that this is a sophisticated form of tritheism. Such a limited polytheism would enable us to think of the Godhead as a community of persons, but would not have solved our original problem of how to think of the God of monotheism as eternally personal.

We cannot, then, meaningfully attribute personality to the infinite and eternal existence of God *a se*. But on the other hand, God is the ground, or creator, or source of personal life, and is in that sense "more" rather than "less" than a person. Further, God is experienced by finite persons as (though not only as) the divine Thou existing over against them in I-Thou relationship. God is personal, then, in the sense that man's awareness of God as Person is a genuine encounter with the transcendent ground of all existence, including personal existence. Using another language, God experienced as personal is a valid transformation in human consciousness of informational input from the transcendent divine source. But we have to add the significant fact that God has been and is experienced by human beings not only as a person but as a number of different persons, each constituted by God's impingement upon a different human community with its own divine image formed through a particular strand of history. Thus the God of Israel is a specific personal deity with his own historical biography. His personal life—that is, his interactions with a group of finite persons—began with his self-revelation to Abraham and has continued in Jewish religious experience down to the present day. As such he has a distinctive personality, developed in interaction with his chosen people: he is a part of their history and they are part of his. And he is a recognizably different personality from, say, the Lord Krishna, because Krishna exists in relation to a different community, forming and formed by a different culture, and creating and created by a different history. Again, the God who speaks to mankind in the Koran is part of yet another history of divine-human relationship. I suggest that this pluralistic situation is rendered intelligible by the hypothesis of one infinite divine noumenon experienced in varying ways within different strands of human history, thereby giving rise to different divine personalities who are each formed in their interactions with a particular community or tradition.

But God is also nonpersonal. We have to affirm this both in the negative sense that personality is a function of personal interaction and therefore cannot be attributed to the eternal divine nature *a se*, and in the positive sense that God is validly experienced in nonpersonal as well as in personal ways. The varying divine personalities worshiped in their respective religious traditions, and likewise the varying nonpersonal forms in which God is known in yet other religious traditions, are all alike divine phenomena formed by the impact of God upon

the plurality of human consciousness. I have concentrat-
ed here upon the awareness of God as personal; but the
other aspect, which I must reserve for later treatment, is
equally important.

It will be evident that the above is a significantly
different hypothesis from one with which it nevertheless
has a partial resemblance, namely the Hindu advaitic
view that God, or Brahman, is nonpersonal, being known
as such in the state of full enlightenment, and that the
worship of personal gods belongs to a lower and preliminary stage of the religious life which is eventually to be
left behind. In distinction from this I am suggesting that
God is to be thought of as the divine noumenon, experienced by mankind as a range of divine phenomena
which take both theistic and nontheistic forms.

At first sight the distinction between divine noumenon
and divine phenomena might seem to preclude any
"doctrine of God," or account of the divine nature. For if
we only know God as experienced by mankind, and if
God is so experienced in a number of different ways,
does not the noumenal or real God remain impenetrably
hidden from us? Thus Feuerbach attacked the distinction between "God as he is in himself and God as he is
for me" as a skeptical distinction. (*The Essence of Christianity*, p. 17; Harper & Row, Harper Torchbook edi-
tion.) And it is true that, on this view, we have to accept
that the infinite divine reality is only knowable by man
insofar as it impinges upon finite human consciousnesses, with their variously limited and conditioned
capacities for awareness and response. But once we
accept this, then the very plurality and variety of the
human experiences of God provide a wider basis for
theology than can the experience of any one religious
tradition taken by itself. For whereas we can learn from
one tradition that God is personal, as the noumenal
ground of theistic experience, and from another tradition
that God is the nonpersonal Void, as the noumenal
ground of its form of mystical experience, we learn from

the two together that God is the ground and source of both types of experience and is in that sense both personal and nonpersonal.

If we now ask, from within the basic religious conviction, why God should be known in such variously imperfect ways, the answer must, I think, hinge upon the fact of finite freedom and the variety of forms which human life has taken in the ramifying exercise of this freedom. We have to consider the difference between, on the one hand, being conscious of the world and of other human beings and, on the other hand, being conscious of God.

We are not diminished in our essential freedom by being aware of the existence of entities below ourselves in the scale of value or of reality. For although the power of storm and earthquake, or the strength of elephant or tiger, dwarfs my own strength, and the vastness of the universe around us reveals us by comparison as microscopically small, yet humanity nevertheless transcends the whole world of nature, with all its immensity and power, by the very fact of consciousness of it. As Pascal said, "If the universe were to crush him, man would still be more noble than that which killed him, because he knows that he dies and the advantage which the universe has over him; the universe knows nothing of this" (*Pensées*, No. 347). And again in relation to other human beings, while many are more intelligent, or more wealthy, or more powerful, etc., yet they are still in the end only fellow mortals, and thus ultimately on the same level as myself. But on the other hand, in relation to that which has absolute reality and value, I am nothing and can have no personal being and freedom in relation to it unless the infinitely valuable reality permits me largely to shut it out of my consciousness. Thus we preserve our freedom over against the infinite reality which, as absolute value, makes a total claim upon us, by being aware of it in terms of limited and limiting concepts and images.

Religious awareness is in this respect continuous with our awareness of other aspects of our environment. For our cognitive machinery, consisting in our sense organs and neurosystem together with the selecting and organizing activity of the mind/brain, has a twofold function: to make us aware of certain aspects of our environment and at the same time to preserve us from being aware of other aspects of it. Shutting out is as important as letting in. It begins in our sensory equipment, which is selectively sensitive only to a minute proportion of the total range of information flowing from our physical environment—only a very small fraction, for example, of the full range of light and sound and other waves which are impinging upon us all the time. And it is essential to our survival and well-being that this should be so. If, for example, instead of seeing water as the continuous shiny substance that we drink, we perceived it as a cloud of electrons in rapid swirling motion, and the glass which holds it as a mass of brilliantly colored crystals, themselves composed of particles in violent activity, we should be bewildered by such an excess of information and should be unable to react appropriately. And so both senses and mind/brain select, and then relate and organize, within the framework of well-tried categories and patterns, with the result that we perceive a version of the world which is enormously simplified and yet such that we can inhabit it successfully.

This need to shut out many aspects of reality in order to live as the finite creatures that we are, not only limited but limited in our specifically human ways, also applies, I have been suggesting, to our consciousness of God. We have a system for filtering out the infinite divine reality and reducing it to forms with which we can cope. This system is religion, which is our resistance (in a sense analogous to that used in electronics) to God. The function of the different religions is to enable us to be conscious of God, and yet only partially and selectively, in step with our own spiritual development, both communal and individual.

It is important to remember that religious traditions,

considered as "filters" or "resistances," function as totalities which include not only concepts and images of God, with the modes of religious experience which they inform, but also systems of doctrine, ritual, and myth, and art forms, moral codes, life-styles, and often patterns of social organization. For religions are communal responses to God, rooted in the life of societies and forming an important, indeed often a dominant, aspect of their culture. Accordingly the spread of religions through missionary activity has usually also been the spread of their associated cultures; and the contemporary phenomenon of individuals being converted from one religion to another while remaining within their original culture— so that, for example, we have Buddhist, Hindu, and Muslim converts within Western societies—is a new and confusing, though perhaps creative, development.

Let us now look, in the briefest possible way, at the application of this broad interpretative conception to the religious history of mankind. Man is a thoroughly historical creature, living through a changing continuum of contingent circumstances into which he has emerged from a primitive prehistoric condition which itself evolved out of lower forms of life. Thus the human awareness of God must be expected to have undergone development through changing historical circumstances, the cumulative growth of traditions, and the influence of those outstanding individuals, prophets and saints, who have in their own individual freedom been more open to God than the societies of which they were members. The influence of such spiritual and moral leaders is crucial; for we are not looking at a natural process of evolution but at a *history*, with all the complex and sometimes conflicting contingencies generated by human freedom. In the earliest stages of this history God was reduced in human awareness to the dimensions of man's own image, so that the gods were, like human kings, often cruel and bloodthirsty; or to the dimensions of the tribe or nation, as the symbol of its unity and power; or again to the more ample dimensions of the forces of nature, such as the life-giving and yet burning radiance of the sun, or the destructive power of storm and earthquake, or the mysterious pervasive force of fertility—and the response that was required, the way of life which such awareness rendered appropriate, was a communal response. The anthropologists have taught us how closely knit primitive societies have been and how little scope they offered for individual thought, whether in religion or in other aspects of life. It was only with the gradual emergence of individuality, in what Jaspers has called the axial period, particularly from about 800 B.C., that higher conceptions of God developed, in correlation with a deeper sense of a moral claim upon human life. For it was the emergence of the individual, and in particular of the religious individual, that made possible the outstanding spiritual leaders on whose consciousness God impinged in new ways or with new intensity and power. The greatest of these became the founders of continuing religious traditions—Moses, Zoroaster, Confucius, Gautama, Jesus, and later Muhammad. Others effected important developments within existing traditions—the Hebrew prophets; the writers of the Upanishads, of the *Tao Te Ching,* and of the *Gita;* Pythagoras, Socrates, Plato, Guru Nanak. These great traditions have continued to develop in larger and smaller ways through the centuries, ramifying out into the vast and complex ideological organisms which we know as the world religions. These religions are thus based upon different human perceptions of, and embody different human responses to, the infinite reality of God.

Let me now end by pointing forward to the next major question that arises if one opts for some such hypothesis as this. I have just referred to the different world religions, with their different images of God. Our question concerns the relative adequacy or value of these different images, both theistic and nontheistic. For it is clearly possible that they are not all equally adequate, but that

some mediate God to mankind better than others. Indeed, to take examples from the Judeo-Christian scriptures, it would be hard to maintain that the image of God
as a bloodthirsty tribal deity urging the Israelites to
slaughter their neighbors (Deut. 7:16), and the image of
God conveyed in Jesus' parable of the prodigal son (Luke
15:11–32), are equal in validity or adequacy or value. But
by what criteria do we assess such images, and how do
we establish such criteria?

We saw early in this chapter that it would be unreason-
able for any religion to claim to be alone authentic,
dismissing all the others as false. But it is entirely
possible that more adequate and less adequate images of
God operate within different religious traditions. How
are we to evaluate these images? This is the large and
difficult question that remains.

VII
Christian Belief
and Interfaith Dialogue

Dialogue, or discussion, between people of different faiths takes place on various levels and in a variety of contexts. There is, first, discursive theological dialogue, concerned with the truth claims of the different religions. But this should always broaden out to include ways of life and forms of art and symbolism, and it should involve opportunities to observe or even participate in one another's religious life at its focal point of worship and contemplation. Here it may begin to pass into a second form of dialogue, the interior dialogue, practiced and reported by such Christian pioneers as the late Père H. le Saux (Swami Abhishiktananda) and Dom Bede Griffiths in India. And then, third, there is the more immediately practical dialogue concerned with common human problems and exemplified, for example, by the Buddhist-Christian-Hindu-Jewish-Muslim discussions at Colombo in 1974, whose report is entitled *Towards World Community: Resources and Responsibilities for Living Together.*

I shall be concerned here primarily with discursive dialogue, though with the understanding that this may pass naturally into the deeper interior dialogue, and also that a common concern about world community is a very proper part of the agenda of interreligious dialogue today, and one to which I shall return at the end of this chapter.

Discursive or theological dialogue, then, takes place

somewhere on or moving about within a spectrum which ranges between two opposite conceptions of its nature. At one extreme there is purely confessional dialogue, in which each partner witnesses to his own faith, convinced that this has absolute truth while his partner's has only relative truth. At the other extreme is truth-seeking dialogue, in which each is conscious that the transcendent Being is infinitely greater than his own limited vision of it, and in which the partners accordingly seek to share their visions in the hope that each may be helped toward a fuller awareness of the divine Reality before which they both stand. Dialogue sometimes takes place nearer to one pole and sometimes nearer to the other, but often varies in character as it proceeds, moving back and forth along the scale.

I

Let us look first at the confessional end of the dialogical spectrum. Here the Christian, in dialogue with people of other faiths, speaks from within his own conviction that God has entered decisively into human history in the person of Jesus Christ, the second Person of the holy Trinity incarnate, who has revealed the divine nature and purpose for man in a unique and unsurpassable way in comparison with which all other revelations must necessarily be secondary, in the sense of being incomplete, or imperfect, or preliminary, or in some other way vitally inferior to the Christian revelation.

This confessional attitude to other religions derives in recent theology from the massive dogmatic work of Karl Barth (particularly the relatively early Barth of *Church Dogmatics*, I/2) and the detailed application of this to the world religions by the great Dutch missionary scholar Hendrik Kraemer in his immensely influential book *The Christian Message in a Non-Christian World*, written for the World Missionary Conference at Tambaram, near

Madras, in 1938. So long as this stance was dominant within the World Council of Churches, as it was until the end of the general secretaryship of Dr. Visser 't Hooft in 1966, this great ecumenical vehicle refrained from inter-religious dialogue. Since then, however, dialogue has become the order of the day, and instead of a confessional rejection of dialogue we have now a confessional stance within dialogue. For those who adopt this stance, the Christian revelation is not one among several, but is the only true revelation of God. This has recently been articulated as follows by the distinguished missionary theologian, Bishop Lesslie Newbigin:

> A Christian who participates in dialogue with people of other faiths will do so on the basis of his faith. The presuppositions which shape his thinking will be those which he draws from the Gospel. This must be quite explicit. He cannot agree that the position of final authority can be taken by anything other than the Gospel—either by a philosophical system, or by mystical experience, or by the requirements of national and global unity. Confessing Christ—incarnate, crucified and risen—as the true light and the true life, he cannot accept any other's alleged authority as having right of way over this. He cannot regard the revelation given in Jesus as one of a type, or as requiring to be interpreted by means of categories based on other ways of understanding the totality of experience. Jesus is—for the believer—the source from whom his understanding of the totality of experience is drawn and therefore the criterion by which other ways of understanding are judged. ("The Basis, Purpose and Manner of Inter-Faith Dialogue," *Scottish Journal of Theology*, Vol. 30, No. 3, 1977, p. 255)

From this point of view the Christian, however personally open and charitable toward people of other faiths, is necessarily bearing witness, or confessing his faith, and he is bound to hope that his hearers will respond to the Word of God which reaches them through his words, and commit themselves to Christ as the way, the truth, and the life. Thus Bishop Newbigin says that the Christian's purpose in entering into dialogue with people of other faiths "can only be obedient witness to Jesus Christ. Any other purpose, any goal which subordinates the honor of Jesus Christ to some purpose derived from another source, is impossible for the Christian. To accept such another purpose would involve a denial of the total lordship of Jesus Christ. A Christian cannot try to evade the accusation that, for him, dialogue is part of his obedient witness to Jesus Christ" (p. 265). Here we see the confessional position adopted as an explicit stance within dialogue.

Needless to say, there is an equivalent confessional stance for the adherents of any other of the religions and ideologies. It is important to keep this fact in mind, because while from within a particular confessional circle of faith one has the impression of standing at the center of the world of meaning, with all other faiths dispersed around its periphery, from the point of view of global history it is evident that there are many different circles of faith, with the inhabitants of each living under the same impression of their own unique centrality. Let us, then, briefly take note of this plurality of centers by referring to Islam, as another Semitic faith; to advaitic Hinduism, as representing a very different kind of religion; and to Marxism, as a powerful secular rival to the traditional religions.

The confessing Muslim, in interreligious dialogue, will speak from within his own faith that Islam represents the latest and fullest revelation, taking up and completing the earlier revelations through Moses and the prophets down to and including Jesus. He will see much good in other religions, particularly in Judaism and Christianity as kindred religions of the Book; but it will be his firm conviction that Islam is the final revelation; and he will inevitably hope that in confessing his faith he may be the instrument of Allah in leading others to commit themselves to the living relationship to God which is Islam.

Again, the Hindu who adheres to the truth revealed in the Vedas and Upanishads as interpreted in the advaitic tradition will speak with people of other faiths from within his conviction that the absolute Reality is beyond all human categories, and that the worship of a personal God occurs on a lower and preliminary level of the religious life. He will see all religions as paths toward the final good of union with the Ultimate, but will see these paths as eventually converging upon the direct way revealed in Advaita Vedanta. Unlike the Christian and the Muslim, however, he will not feel obliged to try to press his own spiritual knowledge upon others, for he believes that they will accept it for themselves when they are ready for it—if not in this life, then in some future life.

Then there is the Marxist in dialogue with religious believers. Whether Marxism is to be accounted a religion is a matter of definition. Personally I prefer a definition of "religion" which involves an essential reference to the Transcendent and which consequently does not include Marxism. Nevertheless, Marxism borders on the religions in that it is a systematic interpretation of human existence which issues in a distinctive way of life; and as such it constitutes one of the most powerful options among the world's living religions and ideologies. And when a Marxist engages in dialogue with people of other faiths than his own he does so from within his conviction that Marxism teaches the truth about man and his history, including the truth that man's religions are projections of human hope, whose historic function has been to enable the exploited masses to bear their servitude patiently rather than rise up against their oppressors. And it must be his hope that through his proclamation of Marxist truth his hearers will be converted and enlisted among the forces of progress.

When these four come together in confessional dialogue, each must in the end be bearing witness to his own faith. But it may be that each is also of an open-minded and inquiring disposition, desirous of learning as well as of bearing witness. They will then come to know about one another's convictions and will be able to compare the different features of their respective belief systems. But still, insofar as they hold to the absolute truth of their own traditions, each will be basically concerned to try to bring the others to share his own faith.

For example, the Christian may enunciate what has traditionally been regarded as the central truth of his faith, namely that Jesus Christ was God the Son incarnate. The Muslim will respond that Jesus was indeed the greatest of the line of prophets before Muhammad himself; and he will acknowledge that Jesus was born of a virgin mother, as the scriptures say. But he will insist that it would be blasphemy to hold that he was actually and literally God, in the sense of being one of the three Persons of a divine Trinity. The Hindu will say that Jesus was indeed a divine incarnation, one of the series of avatars which continues down perhaps to Sri Ramakrishna and Mahatma Gandhi in the nineteenth and twentieth centuries. And the Marxist will say that since God is an illusion, it must be an illusion to think that Jesus was in any sense God incarnate. He was rather a great moral revolutionary whom the church has captured and used for its own counterrevolutionary purposes.

And so long as they all stand firmly within their own respective circles of faith, the dialogue will consist basically in the display and comparison of these incompatible beliefs.

However, interreligious dialogue undertaken just like that, as two (or more) people bearing mutual witness to their own faiths, each in the firm conviction that his is the final truth and in hope of converting the other, can only result either in conversion or in a hardening of differences—occasionally the former but more often the latter.

In order for dialogue to be mutually fruitful, lesser changes than total conversion must be possible and must be hoped for on both (or all) sides. In principle this is readily acknowledged by many contemporary Christian advocates of the confessional stance. Thus Bishop Newbigin says: "We are eager to receive from our partners what God has given them, to hear what God has shown them. In our meeting with men of other faiths we are learning to share in our common patrimony as human beings made by the one God in his own image" (p. 266). He also grants, and indeed affirms, that not only the non-Christian but also the Christian himself should be changed in the course of the dialogue. Indeed he says, "Much of his own 'Christianity' may have to be left behind in this meeting. Much of the intellectual construction, the piety, the practice in which our discipleship of Christ has been expressed may have to be called in question" (p. 268).

Here we approach the living heart of our problem, as it affects the Christian. For the question is, how serious and how radical can this possibility of change be in the Christian partner? Suppose that, in the experience of dialogue, *more* of "the intellectual construction ... in which his discipleship of Christ has been expressed" is called in question than he anticipated? Are there then to be reserved areas of belief which must remain exempt from the possibility of change? May it indeed turn out that he was only playing at openness to change in his own understanding, but that in reality he stood throughout firmly upon a dogmatic conception of what his Christianity must be—a conception which simply corresponded to the traditional structure of Christian orthodoxy?

Let us pursue these questions a little further. In allowing for significant change in the Christian as a fruit of his dialogue with non-Christians it is customary to draw a very important distinction (suggested by that of Karl Barth) between, on the one hand, the historical phenomenon called Christianity, which is one of the religions of the world, and, on the other hand, personal discipleship and devotion to Jesus Christ. This implies an entirely proper and helpful distinction between Jesus—the actual Jesus who lived in Palestine in the first third of the first century, the reports and rumors of whose life and teaching have inspired millions ever since to try to live as his disciples—and the historical development of Christianity, the latter being recognized to be a human, and often all-too-human, affair. And the contemporary confessionalist often suggests that we should engage in dialogue, not primarily as adherents of historical Christianity but simply as disciples of Jesus.

This is, I think, a very fruitful approach. But where it will lead must depend to an important extent upon investigations concerning the historical Jesus, to whom it appeals, and of the ways in which the Christian interpretation of him has been formed over the centuries. The all-important question concerns the extent to which the man Jesus is to be understood in terms of the developed theology of the church. For the confessionalist it is usually an unquestioned assumption that belief in the doctrines of the incarnation and the Trinity are essentially involved in personal discipleship to Jesus. But it is precisely this assumption that has been directly questioned in many recent discussions of Christian origins and of the development of Christian thought, and that is today at the center of a considerable debate. To cite just one major evidence of this, in the 1976 Report of the Church of England's Doctrine Commission, the chairman, in his own essay, wrote that, in using traditional Christian language about Jesus as God's only Son, he is "using language in a very indirect, even poetic, way to express the central role of Jesus in giving form and life to our faith in God" (*Christian Believing*, p. 129); and concerning the doctrine of the Trinity he wrote: "I cannot with integrity say that I believe God to be one in three persons" (p. 126). If the Commission's then chairman, who is also Regius Professor of Divinity at Oxford, can take this view—a view, it should be added, with which some of his colleagues agreed but with which others strongly disagreed—we are clearly in a period of theological reflection in which these doctrines which were once accepted largely without question have now become matters of open debate. And the publication in 1977 of the book *The Myth of God Incarnate* by seven British theologians has opened this debate to a larger public. We can all see at least the possibility that the doctrines of the incarnation and the Trinity may turn out to be part of the "intellectual construction" which has to be left behind when the disciple of Jesus discards the cultural packaging in which Western Christianity has wrapped the gospel.

II

To indicate how this has come about I would remind you that fifty years ago it was widely assumed in Christian circles that Jesus lived his life in the awareness of being God the Son incarnate. It was assumed in much Christian preaching that Jesus knew himself to be divine; that he walked the earth with conscious divine authority, knowledge, and power; and that he taught his own unique divine status in such sayings as "I and my Father are one," "No man cometh unto the Father but by me"; "He that hath seen me hath seen the Father." But that position has become very difficult to sustain in the light of continuing biblical study. It is now widely accepted that the great Christological sayings of the Fourth Gospel express the theology of the church—or at least of an important part of the church—toward the end of the first century; that it is uncertain whether the historical Jesus accepted the designation of Messiah, or Christ; that the meaning of the phrase which he undoubtedly did use of himself, namely, "Son of Man," is still unclear; and that it cannot be established historically that Jesus thought of himself as more than that as which he seems to have been presented in the earliest Christian preaching, namely: "Jesus of Nazareth, a man attested to you by God with mighty works and wonders and signs which God did through him in your midst" (Acts 2: 22). It is accordingly widely acknowledged that if Jesus was indeed God the Son incarnate, he did not know this during his earthly life. Indeed, because of the implausibility of maintaining the divine self-consciousness of the historical Jesus, many are today attracted by the new theory that it was in his resurrection that Jesus either became, or became conscious of being, the Son of God or God the Son.

Such speculations have moved a long way from the original proposition that Jesus of Nazareth presented himself as God the Son living a human life. A further move which many today feel constrained to take acknowledges that the idea of divine incarnation is a poetic or symbolic or mythological way of speaking of God's powerful presence to a faithful human being and through him to others. Whether such a development of Christian understanding is right or wrong is not a matter to be quickly or easily settled, and the current renewed phase of intense Christological discussion may well have to continue for a long time. My own view is that the Christian mind will almost inevitably come to see the doctrine of the incarnation, and the doctrine of the Trinity which grew out of it, in a new way, no longer as precise metaphysical truths but as imaginative constructions giving expression—in the religious and philosophical language of the ancient world—to the Christian's devotion to Jesus as the one who has made the heavenly Father real to him. Or at any rate, I would suggest that this is the kind of development which the more intellectual part of the Christian mind (appropriately, in the human brain, the left hemisphere!) is likely to undergo, while its more emotional other half perhaps continues to use the traditional language of Christian mythology without raising troublesome questions about its meaning. But there may be sufficient overall development for the Christian position in interfaith dialogue to change in character. It may no longer be necessary to insist, however gently, upon the uniqueness and superiority of Christianity; and it may be possible to recognize the separate validity of the other great world religions, and both to learn from them and enable them to learn from the Christian tradition.

This development is continuous with some three centuries of internal change in response to the challenges of modern science and philosophy. Christianity is the first of the ancient world faiths to have attained—however unevenly and falteringly—to a new self-understanding in the light of the scientific revolution; and its gift to the other great religious traditions can now be its own experience of modernization, communicated both in interfaith dialogue and in other ways. This is the role of "critical catalyst" of which Hans Küng has recently written (*On Being a Christian*, pp. 100f.). The Christian responsibility and opportunity are both alike great. For it is for the most part Christian agencies—such as the World Council of Churches' Programme on Dialogue with People of Living Faiths and Ideologies—that are today most actively promoting interreligious dialogue; so that the ethos of the Christian ecumenical movement tends at the same time to set the tone for the wider world ecumenical dialogue.

If it is to fulfill its special role during this new period of religious history, Christianity must, I believe, move emphatically from the confessional to the truth-seeking stance in dialogue. And indeed to a great extent this has already happened, as is shown by the Guidelines for Inter-Religious Dialogue formulated in 1972 by Dr. Stanley Samartha of the World Council of Churches. In this document it is first affirmed: "The basis of interreligious dialogue is the commitment of all partners to their respective faiths and their openness to the insights of the others. The integrity of particular religions must be recognised." This statement acknowledges the degree of validity within the confessional stance, but places it within the context of religious pluralism. It is then said that the objective of dialogue is not a superficial consensus or a dilution of convictions, but "it must lead to the enrichment of all in the discovery of new dimensions of Truth." Finally, after a series of valuable recommendations about the need to go beyond purely intellectual discussion and even to participate in one another's worship, and also to be prepared to take concrete action together for world peace, the document concludes with a statement of the truth-seeking ideal for dialogue: "Inter-religious dialogue should also stress the need to study fundamental questions in the religious dimension of life. Religions are man's responses to the mystery of existence and quests for meaning in the midst of confusion. World religious organisations should support the long-range study of the deeper questions which today ought to be taken up not just separately by individuals of each religion, but also together in the larger interests of mankind." ("The Progress and Promise of Inter-Religious Dialogues," *Journal of Ecumenical Studies*, 1972, pp. 473f.) This seems to me to be the right method and approach.

III

The main impact, in response to which Christianity has undergone the transformations of the last three centuries, is of course that of modern science; and we must ask how the other world religions are likely to respond to the same impact, coming to them from the West in a more powerful form as the impact of an already

formed scientific outlook. Will they be able to survive
the spread among their populations of the scientific
attitude?

We can only speak of probabilities; but the probability
seems to me to be that the other world religions will
survive to about the same extent that Christianity has
survived in the West. For the fact that science first
developed within Christendom does not establish Christianity in an exclusive or proprietary relationship with
the scientific enterprise. Ever since A. N. Whitehead
suggested the idea, in his *Science and the Modern World*
(1925), it has frequently been said that distinctively
Christian theology is responsible for the rise of modern
science by providing the idea of an objective order of
nature waiting to be explored by man. Since the universe
is God's creation, it is said, it must have a rational
structure; and science is the attempt to uncover this
structure. And it does indeed seem reasonable to suppose that the Christian assumption that nature forms an
intelligible system must have constituted one of the
conditions for the rise of science. But that this condition
was not by itself sufficient is shown by the fact that for
the first fifteen centuries of its history Christianity
showed little sign of giving birth to the scientific enterprise. Science, then, can hardly have arisen spontaneous-
ly out of the inner logic of the Christian faith. Further,
the Christian tradition has for much of its history nour-
ished a dogmatic mentality opposed to the freely searching spirit of scientific inquiry; so that for several centuries scientific growth was generally impeded and opposed by the leaders of Christian civilization. Those who
today hail modern science as the glorious child of the
Christian faith may well be great-grandchildren of those
who denounced Charles Darwin as an agent of the devil.
Indeed the general record of the churches in relation to
the rise and progress of modern science, from the time of
Galileo to at least the end of the nineteenth century, has
been so largely negative that what has happened since

then can only be described as a mass conversion!

The origins of the scientific revolution of the sixteenth and seventeenth centuries lie in the many-sided awakening of the European mind from its dogmatic slumbers in the period which is comprehensively called the Renaissance. This was a renaissance of the ancient Greco-Roman civilization, whose literature was spread throughout Europe by the new technique of printing. Science was thus a product of an interaction of cultures. For the rationalistic and inquiring spirit of Greek philosophy seems to have been the main new fertilizing agent which stimulated the rise of modern science in Christian Europe, bringing its medieval phase to an end. And since the scientific enterprise was launched it has generated its own increasing momentum, rapidly establishing its independence from the Christian world view, and indeed continually challenging the Christian faith and forcing it to undergo major transformations in order to remain credible in the light of growing empirical knowledge.

Thus we may say that Christianity provided, unconsciously, an intellectual soil in which the Greek spirit of unimpeded rational inquiry could blossom into the modern scientific outlook, and that this has now in turn largely transformed the intellectual content of Christianity into a faith which does not contradict the findings of the sciences.

It is impossible to know whether, if the course of world history had been different, and something corresponding to the European Renaissance had occurred within one of the civilizations dominated by another world religion, it would have produced the scientific outlook and its practical outworking. For the question which arises concerning the other great world religions is not whether they too can give birth to modern science—for it could only be born once, and this has already happened—but whether they can come to terms with the already formed scientific outlook. So far as technology is concerned, there seems no doubt that this is being successfully exported to many non-Christian cultures, including Hindu India, Buddhist and Shintoist Japan, Maoist China, and some of the Muslim countries of the Middle East. But the deeper question which has yet to be answered is whether the belief systems of these other faiths can assimilate the modern scientific outlook and its results.

The Eastern religions of Hinduism and Buddhism may, I would think, be expected to come to terms with the methods and discoveries of the natural sciences without too much difficulty, and indeed perhaps with rather less trauma than Christianity has experienced. It is true that great parts of India and of the Buddhist lands further east are only now emerging from feudal social conditions resting on a basis of mass ignorance and superstition. But it does not follow from this that Hindu and Buddhist theology must be intrinsically resistant to the development of the modern experimental investigation of the world. That the natural world is *maya* does not mean that it is an illusion in the ordinary sense of that word, but that it is timebound, is in incessant process, and is dependent upon a more ultimate divine reality— this being essentially what Christian theology says when it describes the natural universe as a *contingent* order. Again, the cyclical conception of the universal process is not, as is sometimes said, antiscientific. On the contrary, the notion of a pulsating universe, beginninglessly and endlessly expanding and contracting, is one of the models under discussion in contemporary scientific cosmology. It could turn out that the balance of cosmological evidence and argument will point to the "big bang" being unique, or to its being one of a series, perhaps an infinite series, of moments of compression between contractions and expansions. But science as such does not depend upon a "linear" as opposed to a "cyclical" conception of the process of the universe; the issue will be settled, if it is ever settled, by empirical evidence.

There is, however, another aspect of the scientific

outlook and method which is directly relevant to the world religions and which must seem particularly challenging and threatening to Islam. This is the historical and critical study of ancient literature, including sacred scriptures. Christianity has gone through paroxysms of internal conflict during the last hundred years in breaking away from its former virtually universal assumption concerning the books of the Bible that, to quote a pronouncement of the First Vatican Council, "having been written by inspiration of the Holy Ghost, they have God for their author." Christian scholars now accept that the Bible was written by a variety of human beings over a period of about a thousand years, and that in telling the story of Israel's encounters with God over many generations the biblical writings at the same time express the prescientific assumptions of their authors. Instead of consisting of infallible divine oracles, the biblical writings are the culture-related utterances of men and women of faith as they experienced the divine presence in a variety of historical situations. But to come to this view of the scriptures has been a still-unfinished agony for Christendom.

How will Islam respond to the historicocritical study of the Koran? In one way the problem is less acute than for Christians, in that the Koran has a unitary authorship and was written during a single lifetime; so that the kind of source criticism by which, for example, the Pentateuch and the Synoptic Gospels have been analyzed has little scope in relation to the Koran. But on the other hand the Koran is regarded with even greater veneration by orthodox Muslims than the Bible has ever been by Christians. For it is seen as the Word of God incarnate in human language, as Jesus is seen in orthodox Christian theology as the divine Word incarnate in human flesh. It will therefore not be easy for Muslims to reconcile the divine authority of the Koran, written in seventh-century Arabia, with the modern scientific picture of the universe. It seems likely that in the process there will be a split between Koranic fundamentalists and liberals paralleling, but perhaps deeper and more bitter than, that between Christian fundamentalists and liberals. We must hope that the experience of interfaith dialogue will be helpful to Islam during this difficult period of its history.

IV

Finally, let us turn from the impact of science and technology to the moral and social criticisms and suggestions which the world's faiths may have to offer one another as the interactions between them develop. We can at this point resume the Christian-Muslim-Hindu-Marxist dialogue which we began earlier. This is of course only a segment of the larger and more complex network of world dialogue; and even within this limited segment I am only going to pick out a single question from among the many that will be directed to each of the partners to the dialogue. But this will perhaps serve to illustrate the kind of mutual questioning that is to be expected.

One of the questions put to Hindu India in the dialogue of faiths will concern the caste system—officially rejected in India since 1949 but still in practice persisting in many ways—according to which each individual is born into a particular caste and subcaste which determines his or her occupation, social circle, choice of marriage partner, and spiritual status; and leaving outside the system, with no social or spiritual status at all, the outcastes or untouchables, whom Mahatma Gandhi renamed Harijans, children of God. Is not this a fundamentally unjust system, denying the basic concept of the equality of all mankind? The answer can, surely, only be that this is so. The caste system stands under the same condemnation as feudal social hierarchies, the class structure in many modern Western societies, and the assumption of white superiority and black and brown inferiority which is still so evident among most white Christian populations. But we must remember that in condemning distinctions of caste, class, and color we are speaking from the point of view of a modern liberal concept of human equality which has only recently come to widespread consciousness. If we ask where this immensely important concept has come from, the answer would seem to be that the abstract idea is present in all the major religious traditions, but that its activation as a political force in the world, first in Europe and the United States and then increasingly throughout the world, has resulted from the general undermining of hierarchical authority as a modern has superseded a medieval mentality. India has not yet completed this transition from the medieval to the modern world, and is still in its struggle to throw off the ancient caste system. It must be added that conservative Hinduism continues to be the last stronghold of caste, and that the influence of Christianity, Marxism, and Islam upon Hinduism must be toward the final purging of the blight of caste from the life of India.

One of the questions put to Islam in the multilateral dialogue of faiths will concern the status of women in Muslim societies. The issue here is partly polygamy and partly the traditional subordination of women within patriarchal societies. The respective merits of monogamy and polygamy deserve to be debated in the light of the growing knowledge of human nature offered by psychology and sociology. But polygamy must also be seen in relation to the different stages of social history. Why is it that polygamy was practiced in the societies reflected both in the Koran and in the earlier strata of the Old Testament, but has subsequently died out in Jewish society and is today dying out in Arab societies? It may well be that the liberation of women, which naturally excludes polygamy, is part of a general process of liberation as humanity "comes of age" in the modern world.

But the challenge faces Islam to come to terms with this new outlook, including its effect in liberating women.

One of the major questions put to the Marxists and Maoists in their dialogue with the religions will concern individual human freedom. The religions will have increasingly to recognize a considerable element of truth in the Marxist analysis of the economic dynamics of human society, and a common aim with Marxism in the ideal of a classless society in which men no longer exploit one another. Indeed the moral basis for the criticism both of the Hindu caste system and of polygamy and the traditional subordination of women is most clearly articulated in Marxism. For Marxism embodies in its pure form the mentality produced by the scientific revolution. Marxism is modernity without religion, in contrast to much of contemporary Christianity, which is modernity in a religious form. But the Marxist societies have to face the question whether, in their opposition to capitalist-Christian civilization, they have not themselves become hierarchical and authoritarian, thus negating the concept of human liberation on which they are based. For there are clearly as many features of Marxist as of Christian, Muslim, and Hindu societies which contradict the modern ideal of human equality and freedom.

What questions will the other partners in the ecumenical dialogue put to Christianity? We have seen that the most distinctive feature of the societies of Europe, North America, and Australasia has been that they belong to the modern world. They look across the great gulf of the scientific and technological revolutions to their own medieval past and to the lingering medieval present of many other parts of the world. For Christendom was the civilization within which the transformation of medieval into modern man first took place and through whose influence it is therefore taking place elsewhere. This is Christianity's unique historical role. If we relate the contingencies of history to an overarching divine purpose of creating children of God out of human animals, we can say that it has been Christianity's special vocation to give birth to the modern mentality. But this calling also has its perils and temptations. In being the first science-based culture, Christendom is also the first culture to experience the domination, possibly leading to the destruction, of human life by its own technology. For technology has created the self-consuming consumer society, with its selfish assumption of a continually rising standard of living. This assumption—together with the population explosion made possible by medical technology—is rapidly exhausting the earth's basic mineral and energy resources and creating the prospect of ecological disaster, perhaps in the early decades of the next century. Western civilization may thus be in process of strangling itself by its own unbridled lust for ever greater wealth and luxury; or may indeed destroy itself abruptly in a massive thermonuclear exchange in which the deeply ingrained Western habit of violence puts the marvels of modern technology to suicidal use. Christianity has so far offered no effective resistance to this trend, but is on the contrary deeply implicated in the self-destructive lifestyle and violent tradition of modern Western man. The question is now whether Christian civilization, having become the first bearer of the modern scientific spirit, can avoid being so dominated and corrupted by it that it leads the whole world to destruction.

I am not going to end with any ringing statement of confidence that mankind will succeed in overcoming its immense problems—with the Islamic, Hindu, and Buddhist worlds making their transition from a medieval to a modern mentality without succumbing to the dangers so evident in the West; with the Marxist and Maoist civilizations developing their own forms of personal freedom and creativity; and with the Christian West learning nonviolence from the profoundly peaceful tradition of Buddhism, and learning a certain detachment from material possessions from traditional Hindu wisdom. I do not profess to know whether any of these things will happen. But what can be said with assurance is that each of the great streams of faith within which human life is lived can learn from the others; and that any hope for the future lies largely in the world ecumenical dialogue which is taking place in so many ways and at so many levels.

Index

Since the whole book is about God, and since the word "God" appears throughout, it is not separately indexed.